Berlin in the Cold War

The Battle for the Divided City

Thomas Flemming

berlin edition

Bibliografische Information
der Deutschen Bibliothek
Die Deutsche Bibliothek verzeichnet diese
Publikation in der Deutschen Nationalbiblio-
grafie; detaillierte bibliografische Daten sind
im Internet über http://dnb.ddb.de abrufbar.

© edition q im be.bra verlag GmbH
Berlin-Brandenburg, 2009
KulturBrauerei Haus S
Schönhauser Allee 37, 10435 Berlin
post@bebraverlag.de
Editor: Martin Regenbrecht, Berlin
Translation: Penny Croucher, London
Layout: typegerecht, Berlin
Type: Excelsior 9/12,5 pt, Folio
Printing and subsequent treatment:
Bosch Druck, Landshut
ISBN 978-3-8148-0166-7

www.bebraverlag.de

Contents

American troops escort a civilian vehicle across Checkpoint Charlie

Showdown at Checkpoint Charlie

On the morning of 25th October 1961, American tanks thundered through the West Berlin borough of Kreuzberg and took up position at the Checkpoint Charlie border crossing. Their turrets were pointed threateningly towards East Berlin. Shortly afterwards, two dozen Soviet T–54 tanks moved in from the east to oppose them and swung their gun turrets towards the American tanks. A ghostly silence prevailed. It was the first confrontation between the two Super Powers since the erection of the Berlin Wall two months previously. The world held its breath, for one thing was clear: if a shot were to be fired, it could mean the beginning of a military dispute between the USA and the Soviet Union – with unforeseeable consequences, leading perhaps to a nuclear war which would transform Germany and the whole of central Europe into a contaminated wasteland. US President Kennedy and Party Leader Nikita Khrushchev were kept informed about the explosive situation at Checkpoint Charlie.

The crisis was triggered by an incident at Checkpoint Charlie. Allan Lightner, an American employee at the US Mission in West Berlin, was on his way to the theatre in East Berlin. The GDR People's Police (*Volkspolizei)* at the checkpoint asked him to show his identity card. Lightner refused, because this would have been an infringement of Allied rights, which allowed members of the Occupying Forces to move freely between the sector borders. He returned with a US Military Police escort and was allowed to pass without an identity check. Over the next few days, several other similar incidents occurred until finally, on 25th October, the American tanks took up position. The Western Allies wanted to demonstrate that they insisted on their right to unhindered access to the Soviet sector and that, if necessary, they would defend this right with force.

The confrontation lasted for three days, but it did not come to the worst. On 28th October the Soviet T-54 tanks suddenly withdrew – under direct orders from Moscow and shortly afterwards the American tanks also returned to their barracks. Both heads of state had assured each other that they definitely wanted to avoid an escalation in Berlin. Later when speaking to a journalist, Khruschev summed up the situation very succinctly: "If the tanks had advanced, it would have meant war. If they retreated, it meant peace."[1] They retreated.

Berlin in the front line

October 1961 was certainly neither the first nor the last time that Berlin was the focus of attention in the East-West conflict which was to bring mankind several times to the brink of a Third World War. By 1947 the Allies who had come together to fight against Hitler's Germany were bitter enemies and the four sector city of Berlin was repeatedly the centre stage for the power struggle between the USA and the Soviet Union, which soon became known as "The Cold War".

In June 1948, in order to gain possession of the whole of the former German capital, the Soviet Union set up a blockade and tried to force the Western Allies of Great Britain, France and the USA to withdraw from the three western sectors. For eleven months West Berlin was cut off from the rest of the world and the Western Allies had to airlift in all supplies until Moscow gave up its plan and opened up the road and rail links from West Germany to Berlin.

Four years later, on 17th June 1953, a spontaneous people's uprising against the SED regime broke out in East Berlin which spread to almost the whole of the GDR and it was only by deploying Soviet tanks that Ulbricht was able to hold on to power.

The rest of the world watched Berlin closely, waiting to see if the Americans would give military support to the rebellion in the GDR and thus force the collapse of the SED regime. The Americans held back and the division of power and zones of influence remained untouched in Berlin, as it did in the rest of Europe.

However, Berlin continued to be one of the main areas of conflict in the Cold War.

In November 1958 Moscow proclaimed the so-called "Khruschev Ultimatum" making a renewed demand for the Western Allies to withdraw from Berlin. At the same time, the Soviet Foreign Minister, Andrei Gromyko, even openly threatened that Berlin could turn into a "second Sarajevo", meaning that it could trigger a Third World War in the same way that the assassination in Sarajevo in 1914 of the heir to the Austrian throne had set off the First World War.

In August 1961 Berlin was once more all over the front pages of the world press when the SED regime erected a wall through the middle of the city in order to halt the mounting flood of refugees. On hearing the news from Berlin, US President Kennedy is recorded as saying: "Not a very pleasant solution, but a wall is a damned sight better than a war."[2]

These historical words, which were not published until later, clearly show how close the world came to the brink of war.

War or peace was again the big question in Berlin and in August 1961 the Cold War did not escalate further. Instead the Berlin population paid a high price for this precarious peace lived out in the shadow of the Wall; plans for the future were destroyed and families were torn apart. For the people of East Berlin and the GDR the West was completely blocked off, apparently for good.

Berlin was still in the front line of the Cold War, only now this front consisted of concrete and barbed wire.

The Cold War even ended in Berlin – with the fall of the Wall on 9th November 1989. Berlin witnessed not only many of

A member of the Red Army directing traffic in Ebertstraße

the crises during the Cold War but also its end, which set the seal on German Unification in 1990 and the final withdrawal of all Russian troops from Germany in 1994.

This Cold War was conducted on several fronts in Berlin. It wasn't always a matter of tanks and missiles, but more the danger of a direct military confrontation. This involved the numerous spy missions by which the Secret Services in both the West and the East tried to undermine the position of their opponents.

Berlin therefore became the playground for spies and agents whose activities, as far as we know, sometimes took on grotesque forms.

There was another sense in which Berlin provided the setting for the Cold War because peaceful methods were also used to gain supremacy in the East-West con-

flict. Especially in the 1950s, when Berlin had not yet been divided by the Wall and it was still possible for people to move relatively freely between the sectors, there was an ambitious "battle between political systems".

Here it wasn't just a question of military might but which system could offer the better standard of living and the more comprehensive social services, which had the more modern architecture and the higher quality of cultural life.

In addition, Berlin was not least an experimenting ground for détente. The periods of confrontation and high risk of war, for example the blockade in 1948, the building of the Wall in 1961 or the Khrushchev Ultimatum, were often followed by discussions and negotiations whose aim was to make life easier for

Oberbaum Bridge with the sector border sign in four languages

the Berliners in spite of the Wall and the barbed wire.

For example, the pass permit regulations and the 1971 Berlin Treaty made the wall more permeable and gradually defused the Berlin powder keg.

The Cold War in Berlin was a multi-layered and fascinating epoch which produced a large number of dramatic confrontations and daily conflicts and at the same time periods of astonishing normality.

Allies become enemies

On 2nd May 1945 the remaining units of the German Wehrmacht surrendered to the Soviet forces. In hard fought battles and with heavy losses. the Red Army had conquered and finally occupied the German capital. Six days later on 8th May 1945, the German Wehrmacht commanders signed the unconditional surrender of all German forces in Berlin-Karlshorst. Nazi Germany and its armed units, which had committed monstrous crimes during the Second World War, had been finally defeated.

This victory had only become possible because of the alliance created between the USA, Great Britain and the Soviet Union. However these Allies, who found themselves thrown together after Nazi Germany invaded the Soviet Union in June 1941, were very different animals: Great Britain, the cradle of democracy; the USA, a democratic economic giant and the Soviet Union, the "third Ally" presided over by the dictator, Josef W. Stalin. Any reservations and mistrust between the Western democrats and the communist Soviet Union were put aside by their politicians in order to achieve one aim – the defeat of Nazi Germany.

This aim was achieved in May 1945. The German Reich had surrendered unconditionally and the whole of Germany was occupied by Allied troops. The "Big Three" had held several summits and reached agreement on the essential features of the subsequent occupation policy. They met in Teheran (1943), in Yalta in the Crimean peninsula (February 1945) and in Potsdam (August 1945). In line with these discussions, the areas east of the Oder and the Neiße were added to Poland or the Soviet Union (north-east Prussia and Königs-

berg) and the remainder of Germany was divided into four zones of occupation, as France joined the Allies as the fourth occupying power. The victorious Allies were even able to agree on the basic principles of their occupation policy relatively quickly. They decreed that German society should be 1. denazified, 2. demilitarised and 3. "democratised". However, what this "democratisation" was meant to actually look like and how it was to be managed was soon hotly disputed among the Allies.

The highest government power in the individual zones of occupation lay with the respective military governments with a Military Governor at the helm. They controlled all political, economic and cultural matters in their zone as they wished.

Any matters which affected "Germany as a whole" were dealt with by an "Allied Control Council" *(Alliierter Kontrollrat)* in Berlin where all four Military Governors sat round one table and at first it seemed as if the Americans, British, French and Soviets were working together relatively harmoniously.

The four sector city

As former capital of Germany, Berlin was also divided into four zones of occupation by the victorious powers, in this case called "sectors". The British had the western districts (Wilmersdorf, Charlottenburg, Spandau, Tiergarten), the Americans had the south-west (Kreuzberg, Schöneberg, Neukölln, Tempelhof, Steglitz, Zehlendorf), the French the north-west (Reinickendorf, Wedding) and the Soviet Occupying Powers had the eastern boroughs of Berlin (Mitte, Prenzlauer Berg,

Marshal Shukow (with sash) and Field Marshal Montgomery (3rd from right) at a military parade

Weißensee, Lichtenberg, Friedrichshain, Treptow, Köpenick). The three West sectors comprised an area of 481 square kilometres with 2.1 million inhabitants (1945) and the Soviet sector was 403 square kilometres with 1.1 million inhabitants. The sector boundaries were simply marked out by occasional road signs and people could move unimpeded between the sectors. In accordance with the London Treaty of September 1944, which also decided on the basic features of occupation policy in Germany, a joint government was set up to control the four sector city of Berlin.

The highest decision making committee was the "Allied Kommandatura" (a combination of an English and a Russian concept), where the four City Commandants were represented. It was based in the wealthy Berlin district of Dahlem in the American sector and met for the first time on 11th July 1945.

From the middle of July 1945, with its four zones or "sectors" and Allied Control Council or "Allied Kommandatura", Berlin was in the form and structure of its governance under occupation a kind of "mini-Germany" which soon became the stage for the conflicts of the Cold War.

First conflicts

Even while the final battles were still raging in Berlin, ten members of the KPD (German Communist Party) who had been preparing for this moment in exile in Moscow, moved into the city to start organising the reconstruction of Berlin. These men were called the "Gruppe Ulbricht" after their leader Walter Ulbricht, who

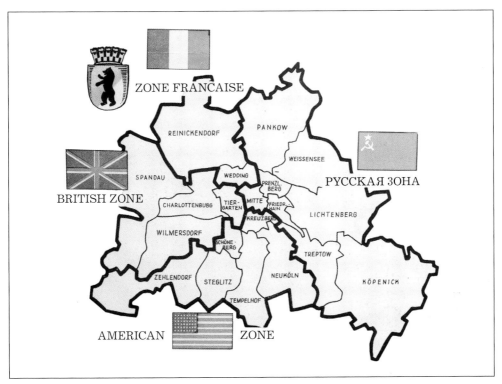

Map of the sector borders

later became the State and Party leader of the GDR (German Democratic Republic). As the Red Army had conquered the German Capital on their own it was not until several weeks later that the Western Allies were able to move into their respective sectors, the Americans and British in July and the French in August 1945. In the meantime the Ulbricht Group, with support from the Soviets, were free to set the political course which was to lead to increasingly fierce conflicts with the Western Allies.

They had, for example, seen to it that several key positions in the City Council (*Magistrat*) were occupied by their own people. One member of the group, Kurt Maron, obtained the highly influential position of First Deputy to the Mayor, Arthur Werner, a retired architect with absolutely

no experience of politics. The aim was not necessarily to fill all the posts with communists and to gear everything towards the speedy introduction of a Soviet style socialist system, but Ulbricht and his associates wanted to have a crucial influence on political development in Berlin and the Soviet zone of occupation.

One of Walter Ulbricht's often quoted remarks was: "It must look democratic, but we must have everything in our hands".[3] To start with, therefore, they deliberately sought to co-operate with social democrats and middle class conservatives because in the immediate aftermath of the war the "anti-fascist democratic revolution" was the first priority even for communists in the Walter Ulbricht mould, despite the fact that he had, secretly, stated that "we must have everything under our own control." Whilst Ulbricht's communists in the east sector could always count on the support of the Soviet occupying powers or even carried out their directives, they soon met with increasing resistance in the west sectors of Berlin.

Before the Western Allies arrived, in matters of industrial installations and reparations the Soviets had already created a *fait accompli* which contained serious potential for conflict. As soon as the war was over they had actually sent in special detachments to dismantle large amounts of industrial plant of which in the west part of the city, later the west sectors, 80 per cent of industrial capacity was affected, whereas in the Soviet Sector it was "only" a third. When the Western Allies took over their sectors in the summer of 1945, they therefore found that the industrial landscape was largely destroyed. Any machinery and industrial plant that remained after the bombing and street battles had mostly been removed by the Soviet special detachments. The fact that only a tiny proportion of these machines arrived back in the Soviet Union in one piece and that the dismantling policy proved to be economically completely senseless for the Soviet Union is another matter.

It has to be said that the Western Allies, especially the French, also dismantled some of the industrial plant in their sectors, but it was nothing in comparison to the devastating extent to which the Soviets destroyed the industrial reserves. Towards the end of 1945 the Soviets turned some of the most successful businesses in their sector (which had not been dismantled) into "Soviet Joint-stock Companies" *(Sowjetische Aktien-Gesellschaften SAG)*, which had to produce goods exclusively for the Soviet Union – a direct violation of the agreements about a joint economic policy.

With regard to the provision of food and raw materials, the Soviets insisted that the western sectors should be supplied by their respective occupied zones. This meant that the city boroughs in the West Berlin were actually cut off from their hinterland in Brandenburg.[4]

The founding of political parties

It would probably surprise many people how quickly and (apparently) generously the Soviet Occupying Power in Berlin and the Soviet Occupation Zone (*SBZ*) got things moving on the political front. Order No.2 allowed the Soviet Commander-in-Chief, Marschall Georgi K. Shukov, to found political parties as early as June 1945. In the days that followed, a group of communists led by Wilhelm Pieck and Johannes R. Becher, published an appeal to found the KPD (German Communist Party).

On 15th June 1945 a committee to (re-) found the SPD (Social Democrats) was constituted with Otto Grotewohl at its head. The key concepts of their appeal were the "democratisation of State and society" as well as the "socialisation of the economy".

On 26th June 1945 there was an appeal to found the CDU (Christian Democratic Union) and on 5th July the LDP (Liberal Democrats). Unlike the KPD and the SPD, these parties were quite new and had no forerunners in the Weimar Republic. The CDU followed the tradition of the centre and the LPD was based on the politics of the DVP (Democratic People's Party) and the DDP (Democratic Party).

These parties started their work in Berlin and the SBZ (Soviet Zone of Occupation) and at this point in time there was no thought of founding or re-founding parties in the western zones of occupation.

It became clear only too soon to what extent the Soviets made sure that these comparatively quickly permitted parties pursued policies that suited them. In November 1945, when the CDU chairman, Andreas Hermes and his deputy, Walther Schreiber, dared to criticise the land reform, in particular the expropriation of large plots of land without any compensation, they were immediately forced to resign. The same thing happened to their successors, Ernst Lemmer and Jakob Kaiser, two years later when they refused to take part in the "People's Congress for unity and just peace", a propaganda event for the communists.

The question of amalgamating the SPD and the KPD also turned into another extremely explosive dispute between the East and the West.

In 1945 many SPD members even felt that the organisational division of the workers' movement fatally weakened their punching power. This division had been one of the reasons why the Weimar Republic had failed and the Nazis had been able to seize power in 1933 and that is why after the war there was a willingness amongst wide sections of Germans as well as Berlin Social Democrats to join forces with the KPD. However, this willingness in the SPD waned all the more rapidly when it became clear that the communists intended to win key positions with Soviet help and to execute their plans with great severity.

Otto Grotewohl, chairman of the SPD in the SBZ ignored these concerns, put opponents of union with the KPD in their place and finally led the SPD into a joint party with the communists, the SED, Social Unity Party of Germany *(Sozialistische Einheitspartei Deutschland)*, and the first official party conference took place on 21st/22nd April 1946 in the Berlin Admiralspalast.

There was particularly strong resistance to amalgamation with the KPD within the Berlin SPD and with support from the Western Allies opponents to the merger organised a ballot. This was held towards the end of March 1946, but could only be conducted in the three West sectors; in the Soviet Sector force was used to prevent it. In spite of a ban, polling stations were set up in the east sector but they were soon shut down by Soviet soldiers and the SPD members who were queueing outside had to go home without being able to cast a vote. The result of the ballot was clear: in the west sectors 75 per cent of the SPD membership was against a merger with the communists.

Their fears were soon to prove well founded. Hardly had the ink dried on the signatures to the amalgamation of the KPD and the SPD, when political pressure started to be exerted on the former Social Democrats within the SED. Using threats and even outright violence, the communists forced numerous Social Democrats out of their positions of power in the SED and determined the political course of the party, just as the Soviet Occupying Power had wanted and with their support. Flimsy accusations were used to remove thousands of former SPD members in the SED from office and some even ended up in prison.[5]

When it came to reconstructing the trade unions which the National Socialists had banned in 1933, in Berlin there was a dispute between communist unionists and moderate groups. Once again the communists had at their disposal a larger number of well schooled officials from exile in Moscow than social-democratic or christian-conservative inclined workers or employees. They also had fewer democratic scruples about accomplishing their aims. The "Free German Workers' Union" *(FDGB)* was therefore dominated by communists and increasingly developed

Walter Ulbricht at the Party convention unifying the KPD and SPD into the SED

into a servant of the SED and the Soviet Occupying Power. However, non-trade unionists succeeded in forming an "Independent Trade Union Organisation" *(UGO)* which despite massive hindrance from the communists gained 32 per cent of the votes in the union elections held in the spring of 1948.

In the west of Berlin, without any help from the Western Allies, the UGO was even able to win 70 per cent of the delegates' seats. When the FDGB subsequently tried to obtain the majority by means of deliberate manipulation, the UGO split from the FDGB in August 1948 and set themselves up in the west sectors as independent liberal-democratic trade union organisations.

The Cold War which was being fought on all levels had also led to a situation where even the trade unions in Berlin had split into two enemy camps.[6]

The last "united Berlin" elections

Despite the increasing tensions between East and West, in October 1946 there were free elections for the city council *(Stadtverordnetenversammlung)* which had authority over the whole of Berlin. These elections were the first since 1932 and the last until 1990. The Allies ensured that democratic regulations were observed, so the voting was free and secret. It was only in the East sector where the SPD's election campaign came up against massive obstructions, including a ban on meetings and confiscation of newspapers and pamphlets.

The result was a clear mandate from the men and women of Berlin for their city to be developed along democratic lines. In a 92.3 per cent turnout the SPD won 48.7 per cent of the votes cast, thereby only just missing a clear majority. Even in the eastern boroughs the Social Democrats achieved over 43 per cent and the SED gained just 30 per cent. The second strongest overall was the CDU with 22 per cent and the SED received only 19.8 per cent.

After this election setback the SED newspaper "Neues Deutschland" commented: "This decision did not occur in favour of the ... political and economic demands (of the SED) and the work we have achieved so far, but as a result of weeks of bias used against the SED by the reactionary press ... Therefore the election result in Berlin should be regarded as a politically wrong decision." This could only be interpreted as an open announcement that the "wrong decision" taken by the Berlin population needed to be reversed as soon as possible. In the east sector, at least, this was eventually to be the case.

Despite its defeat, the SED belonged to the City Council (*Magistrat*) which was newly elected at the beginning of December 1948. They tried to obtain as many posts and offices as possible which in May 1945, without any democratic legitimacy, had been handed over to them by the Soviets. The CDU and SPD, however, which held a broad majority in the parliament, fought against this.

The Soviets vetoed the election of Ernst Reuter as Mayor of Berlin. He was a thorn

Election posters for the city council elections in October 1946

in their side because he was a former communist and in their eyes therefore a renegade. They may have managed to prevent him from taking up office but in doing so they unintentionally turned him into a symbol of democratic resistance against a communist takeover of the whole of Berlin.

Blockade and Airlift

1948, the year of the Berlin Blockade, marked the first crisis in the Cold War in and around Berlin and led to political division. This highly explosive dispute between the Western Allies and the Soviet Union, during the course of which at times the West, at least, considered resorting to the use of atomic weapons, was triggered by the currency reform[7]. However, the deeper reason behind the blockade was the attempt by Moscow to drive the Western Allies from the four sector city and incorporate the whole of Berlin into their power base. Moreover the Soviet Union wanted to use the Berlin blockade to prevent the West's preparations for the creation of a West German "part" State, which would ruin their power political ambitions for the whole of Germany.

Competing currencies

On 20th June 1948, after months of preparations, a currency reform came into force in the three western zones of occupation. The old Reichsmark became invalid and the new currency was the D-mark. The necessity for a change of currency was universally accepted because of galloping inflation and the rampant black-market. All over Germany the economy was in urgent need of a reliable currency. Even the Soviet Union recognised this and after the talks in the Kontrollrat between the four Occupying Powers about a currency reform for the whole of Germany broke down, they then started preparing for a currency reform for their zone as well. On 23rd June 1948 the Soviet Union introduced their own separate currency reform. There was a great deal of controversy surrounding the question of which currency should now be valid in Berlin. Should it be the D-mark or the Ostmark? The Western Allies had specifically excluded their sectors in Berlin from the currency reform in view of the "special agreements which exist for the Four Power Government in this city", as the US Military Governor Lucius D. Clay informed his Soviet counterpart Wassili D. Sokolowski.[8] The Soviets, however, had their own way of interpreting things, which meant that the whole of Berlin including the western sectors were part of the Soviet economy and that therefore the Ostmark ought to be used in the west sectors.

The Western Allies were even prepared to accept this, with the proviso that the currency reform in Berlin would be carried out under the instructions and supervision of the joint Kontrollrat and not just by the Soviet military administration (SMAD) alone. The Soviets, however, rejected this idea. They clearly saw the currency switch as an important step towards completing

Banknotes for the Western sectors of Berlin with "B" stamped on themselves

Queues of people in front of a bureau d'échange in Neukölln

their gain of political power of the whole of Berlin.

On 25th June the Western Allies put a stop to this plan by starting to issue the new money in their sectors. The notes were that same as those which had been issued in the West zones except they had a "B" stamped on them. In addition, the use of the Ostmark was permitted in the west sectors whereas the West Mark could not be used by the Berliners living in the Soviet Sector. This meant that from mid-June 1948 onwards, there were two currencies in West Berlin. However, what appeared on the face of it to be a compromise, was actually the result of a heated confrontation.[9]

"Raisin bombers" (Rosinenbomber) against the blockade

On 24th June 1948 the Soviets blocked all the road, rail and water links between Ber-lin and the west zones and no cars, lorries or trains were allowed through. This meant that the all the land links to the zones in West Germany were completely closed, only the three air corridors remained open. Even the electricity supply was cut off. The Soviets' official explanation was they were directly reacting to the currency reform which had been introduced in West Germany on 20th June. They had been forced to interrupt the flow of traffic between the zones, "to protect the interests of the population and the economy of the Soviet Union as well as to prevent the disorganisation caused by the circulation of the new currency."

In fact, a few months previously, the Soviets had already closed off land routes several times due to alleged "technical faults". On 24th January 1948 a British military train had been stopped at the Marienborn border checkpoint and was not allowed to

A Berlin family without electricity or coal during the blockade

continue its journey and in the weeks that followed it became clear that Moscow was testing the resolve of the Western Allies by means of increasing incidents of hindrance and harassment against their vehicles. The Soviets were now taking revenge for the fact that in 1945 the Western Allies had not come to a binding agreement with them about the land routes to and from Berlin. The only international agreements in existence were on the three air corridors and Stalin evidently intended to adhere to them.

However, the Western Allies were not going to be easily driven out of Berlin and repeatedly insisted on free access to the city by land routes as well.

When the full blockade was imposed on 24th June this access was denied. The Western Allies now had a difficult decision to make. Should they give in to Soviet pressure and give up their position in Berlin? This would inevitably mean that the west

sectors would come under Soviet rule. Or should they insist on their presence in Berlin and thereby run the risk of an exchange of blows which could rapidly turn into a major war between the super powers? Washington's initial reaction was one of helplessness. Spontaneous thoughts of sending vehicle convoys to Berlin under military protection were quickly rejected as this would probably mean the start of a military conflict. So was a retreat necessary – for the sake of sacred peace?

It was the US Military Governor of Berlin, Lucius Clay, who took the initiative to launch a daring operation on 24th June, the very first day of the blockade; if the land routes were blocked then the three Western Sectors of Berlin would have to be supplied by air. With an estimated daily requirement of 10,000 tons of supplies for 2.1 million West Berliners this was an enormous task, but Clay was convinced that it was also

A "raisin bomber" landing at Tempelhof Airport

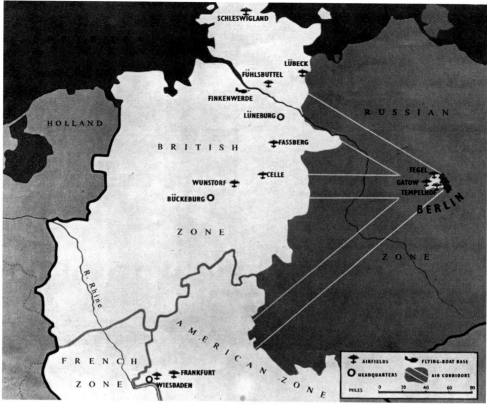

The Allied air corridors secured the delivery of provisions to West Berlin

possible. He immediately requested all available aircraft of the US Air Force for an "airlift" *(Luftbrücke)* in order to supply Berlin with all their needs, from food and medicine to fuel and toys. US President Harry S. Truman gave the green light. Stalin had left a door open – the air corridors. The West now intended to use them and simultaneously keep the conflict with the Soviet Union from escalating into a "war".

On the morning of 25th June, barely 24 hours after the blockade had been declared, the first "C-47 Dakotas", two engined transport aircraft with a 2.5 ton capacity, landed at Tempelhof Airport. Operation "airlift" had begun and over the coming weeks and months it turned into the largest supply operation in history. Initially the daily delivery of supplies amounted to 1,201 tons – a fraction of what was actually needed – but by the beginning of August it had risen to 4,200 tons and by the spring of 1945 the airlift 8,000 tons of supplies were reaching West Berlin every day.

The airlift was planned and implemented with military precision and involved a total of over 500 American and British aircraft using three air routes to Berlin; the north corridor (over Hamburg), the middle corridor (over Hanover) and the south corridor (over Frankfurt). The south corridor was a kind of one way street for flights into Berlin, the middle corridor was for return flights and only the north corridor was used in both directions. As the aircraft were frequently landing at two minute intervals at

The transport aircraft were unloaded at Tempelhof Airport

the West Berlin airports of Tempelhof and Gatow and the provisional airstrip at Tegel, this necessitated a cleverly devised timetable and the use of the very latest technology including radar, which was then still in its first stages of development. An American pilot who took part in the operation recalled: "If a pilot messed up his landing approach for some reason, he had to take off again immediately and leave Berlin through the middle corridor. His flight was wasted – but in those days there was no other way to avoid dangerous tailbacks."[10]

The roar of the aircraft engines became "the sound of hope" for the Berliners and they began disrespectfully but affectionately to call the aircraft themselves "raisin bombers". However, it has to be said that despite the success of the airlift, the blockade remained a time of great sacrifice and hardship for the population in the western sectors of Berlin. The Soviets had also cut off gas and electricity supplies from the east so that power cuts were a daily occurrence. Even coal and other heating fuel had to be flown in which meant that by the beginning of autumn the cold was added to the deteriorating food situation as an even worse factor. "Warm rooms" were set up because private homes could barely be heated. Numerous businesses had to stop production because of lack of materials and energy resulting in a sudden increase in the number of unemployed.

If the blockade was a strategic move by Moscow on the chessboard of world politics

Gathering wood in the Tiergarten

"friends", as they were frequently described in official reports.

Over 300,000 Berliners clearly demonstrated their will for self-determination on 9th September 1948 at a rally in front of the ruins of the Reichstag. The mass demonstration was staged to coincide with the negotiations being held by the four victorious allies in the Berlin Control Council building because many people feared that the Western Powers and Moscow could still find a way out of the blockade crisis, but that it would be at the expense of the western sectors of Berlin. Ernst Reuter, the elected Mayor of Berlin (who the Soviets did not acknowledge), therefore sent a direct fiery appeal to the "peoples of the world": "Today is the day when the people of Berlin raise their voices … In all this trading and negotiating we Berliners do not want to be exchange goods … You peoples of the world, people in America, in England, in France, in Italy! Look at this city! And recognize that you may not and cannot betray this city and this people."

At least Reuter's appeal had an effect on the Western Allies. They stuck firmly to their position with Moscow and expanded the airlift further. They even declared a small "counter-blockade" by shutting off West Berlin to traffic in and out of the Soviet Zone of Occupation which meant, among other things, that the East had to build expensive alternative road and rail routes.

Overall the blockade turned into a political own goal for the Soviet Union. They were unable to realise any of their aims; the Western Allies remained in Berlin and persisted in their legal position with regard to status. The preparations for the foundation of a West German state continued unhindered and finally, as already mentioned, a deep feeling of solidarity had developed between the West Berliners and the powers in the West. From now on, the

in the battle for power and supremacy in Europe, their first and direct victims were the inhabitants of West Berlin. However, they could not be forced to their knees any more than the Western Allies; on the contrary, during the blockade the Berliners developed a political self-determination which was to prove its worth in similar explosive conflicts in the years that followed.

Whatever vague sympathy the West Berliners may have still had for the Soviet Union and communist ideas from the days of the Weimar Republic or the anti-fascist resistance, was totally destroyed by the brutal attempt to use the blockade to take the population of half a city as hostages. On the other hand the airlift markedly improved the relationship between the West Berliners and the Western Allies. The huge financial commitment meant that in 1948/49 the "occupying forces" in West Berlin turned into "protecting powers" or even

East – be it the leadership in the Kremlin or the SED – had not only the Western Powers and the anti-communist politicians in Berlin against them, but also the majority of the population.

With all this in mind, in April 1949 the Moscow leadership showed it was prepared to make concessions. The UN ambassadors for the Soviet Union and the USA consequently met to negotiate lifting the blockade which led to the New York Treaty of 4th May 1949.

During the night of 12th May 1949 the road and rail links to and from Berlin were open once again.

The West Berlin population was able to breathe a sigh of relief after eleven long months during which the western sectors had received all their provisions exclusively by air. The first lorries to arrive were greeted with enthusiastic rejoicing and at last there was enough food, clothing and other daily necessities and the shelves in the shops filled up again. American and British aircraft had made a total of over 200,000 flights into the blockaded city and delivered almost 1.8 million tons of goods, of which just under a third (28 per cent) was food. The highest proportion (63 per cent) was coal and 9 per cent was industrial goods, including the building materials for a complete power station that was erected in Spandau during the blockade in order to improve the energy supply to the Western Sectors.

In July 1951 a memorial to the airlift was unveiled in front of Tempelhof Airport. On its base are carved the names of the 75 Americans, Britons and Germans who lost their lives during the airlift.

The blockade and the airlift had certainly turned Berlin into a political symbol. From now on its name stood for the determination of the Western Powers to stop any attempts at expansion by the Soviet Union, if necessary even by military means.

Berlin City Mayor Ernst Reuter appeals to the "peoples of the world"

The "Senate reserves" (Senatsreserve)

The blockade caused a further curiosity in a West Berlin which was not exactly short of such things.

Nowhere else in the world was there anything like the Senate reserves or Berlin stockpile which were set up on the orders of the Western Allies straight after the end of the blockade.

Thousands of tons of food and consumer goods were stored in 250 secret locations so that West Berlin would be prepared for any future blockade measures. These supplies included preservable groceries (tinned food etc.) clothing, fuel, coal and even bicycles. The amount of goods was measured by how much the West Berlin population would need for six months (one year for some goods). The individual groups of goods,

The Berlin Senate food supplies which were stored as a result of the airlift

especially the groceries, were regularly exchanged for new ones and sold off in the shops.

Despite the enormous costs involved – maintenance and storage alone cost about 100 million DM (about 50 million Euro) per year – the Berlin stockpile continued throughout the years of division. The reserves were not finally dissolved until the reunification of Berlin in October 1990 and herein lay a certain irony as the majority of the food supplies, to the value of approximately 200 million Euros, was delivered to the Soviet Union as humanitarian aid.

The Divided City

On 6th September 1948 communist demonstrators stormed the City Hall (*Neues Stadthaus*), the headquarters of the Berlin City Assembly (*Stadtverordnetenversammlung*). The demonstrators wanted to put pressure on the city parliament, where the SPD and the CDU were in the majority, and prevent the forthcoming elections in December 1948 because of the renewed threat of defeat for the SED. In addition they demanded that the Ostmark be introduced in the west sectors of Berlin as well.

The City Hall was in the east sector of Berlin and so the parliamentary president, Otto Suhr (SPD), asked for protection from the Soviets. When his request was turned down he closed the session and moved the venue to the student headquarters near the Zoological Gardens in the British Sector. The SED members of parliament refused to move and so from now on, the Berlin City Assembly was divided. Since the end of June 1948 tensions had mounted not only between the two super powers of the USA and the Soviet Union but also within the political life of Berlin, which had continued to have a joint parliament and be ruled by the joint City Council (*Magistrat*). In several departments of the City Council the Soviets ordered the dismissal of leading officials who opposed any communist influence. Consequently the departments where the SPD and CDU were in the majority, were moved into the west sectors.

There were also increasing conflicts about the police. Paul Markgraf, the Commissioner who had been placed there by the SED, high-handedly discharged any police officers he didn't want. On 26th July 1948, the incumbent Mayor of Berlin, Ferdinand Friedensburg (CDU), subsequently suspended Markgraf from his post but he refused to go. From the end of July there were two police authorities in Berlin; the West Berlin Police under Acting Commissioner, Johannes Stumm, which contained about 70 per cent of all Berlin police officers, and a police force in the Soviet Sector, led by Markgraf and controlled by the SED.

The SED instituted the next decisive step in the division with a so-called extraordinary City Assembly meeting which convened on 30th November 1948 in the East Berlin Admiralspalast. The participants were the 23 remaining SED members of parliament together with, quite illegally, several hundred representatives of communist controlled organisations such as the FDGB, the Frauenbund (DFB), and the Free German Youth (*Freie Deutsche Jugend, FDJ*). This meeting, which had no democratic legal status, declared the elected City Council deposed and then elected a "temporary democratic City Council". This 1948 *Magistrat* was a perfect example of how the less democratic a committee in the Soviet sector was, the more likely it was to be described as "democratic". The SED politician, Friedrich Ebert, son of the first President of the Weimar Republic, was elected as the head of this SED controlled Council and thus became the new Mayor of Berlin. The Western Allies immediately submitted a protest against this unconstitutional action to the Soviet Occupying Power, which was promptly rejected.

The planned elections to the City Assembly were held a few days later, on 5th December 1948, but only in the west sectors and without any SED candidates. With 64.5 per cent of the votes, the SPD gained a convincing victory. The CDU received 19.4 per

Communist demonstrators storm the City Council (Magistratsgebäude)

cent and the Liberal Democrats (LDP) 16.1 per cent. The SPD politician, Ernst Reuter, was duly elected Mayor again and in view of the extremely difficult political situation *vis à vis* the blockade and the political division of the city, he formed an all-party City Council.

When the "minor occupation status" of 14th May 1949 was introduced, the West Berlin City Council also gained extensive decision making powers which meant that the Allied Kommandantura no longer had exclusive control over the city's future development.

However, the victors still continued to keep some authority, for example in the areas of security and demilitarisation as well as control over the police and banks.

From the end of 1948 onwards there were therefore two competing governments and parliaments in Berlin which each denied the other's legitimacy. The political

and administrative division was complete and the border between the east and the west sectors had become a real front line where the opponents in the Cold War faced each other with increasing mistrust.

The University as a political battlefield

Soon even Berlin University, where teaching had already begun again in January 1946 on the orders of the Soviet Military Administration (SMAD), became the scene of political disagreements between the East and the West.

The University in Unter den Linden, therefore in the Soviet Sector, was subjected to increasing pressure by the Soviets and the SED, both with regard to course content and personnel. Any professors or students who did not want to bow to this influence were harassed and pressured. In March

Inaugural ceremony of the The Free University of Berlin

1947 several students were arrested, most of them members of the SPD or the CDU.

In the spring of 1948 the situation was further intensified when the SED reacted to the students' demands for more freedom in research and teaching by relegating numerous students as well as making massive threats.

Two dozen or so students and lecturers thereupon took the initiative to found an independent university, free of any political influences, in the west of the four sector city. They found support above all from the Americans, in particular from the US Military Governor, Lucius D. Clay, with the result that the new institution was officially founded on 4th December 1948 with the programmatic name "The Free University" and was situated in the idyllic area of Dahlem in the American Sector, only a stone's throw away from the Allied Kommandantura building.

From now on the Cold War in Berlin also manifested itself in the existence of two competing universities. Both the other two higher educational institutions, the Academy of Arts and the Technical University, were in West Berlin and were therefore protected from the East-West confrontation.

Troops in Berlin

The expression "Front-line city" *(Frontstadt)* was a very apt description for the situation in Berlin at this time, because both sides had a massive military presence.

Alongside their job of deterring any possible attack on West Berlin, the western forces also had the task of demonstrating the western powers' legal claim to a permanent presence in Berlin. The Western Allies had, on average, about 12,200 soldiers in Berlin; 6,000 American, 3,600 British and 2,600 French. In the west sectors there were

Allied Forces Victory Parade in 1945

60 tanks, 80 armoured vehicles and six artillery guns, but no fighter aircraft or air defence systems.

On the other side, within a radius of about 30 kilometres, there were about 90,000 troops belonging to the "group of Soviet forces in Germany" and, from 1956 onwards, units of the National Peoples' Army of the GDR. After the building of the Berlin Wall in 1961, there were a further 11,000 men from the Border Troops of the GDR who were deployed on the border fortifications between East and West Berlin.

Meanwhile relations between the occupying powers had been officially severed when the Soviets walked out of the Allied Kommandantura in the middle of June 1948 and rendered it useless as the four power instrument for the administration of Berlin. On 21st December, the three West City Commandants resumed the Allied Kommandantura sessions without a Soviet representative. From now on, they referred to the absence of the Soviets as an "abstention" and not as a "veto" and continued to claim that their resolutions were valid for the whole of Berlin. However, in actual fact these were little diplomatic or legal games because the Soviets doggedly refused to recognise any resolutions made by the Western Allies for the whole of Berlin, let alone implement them in their own sector.

Cutting off the west sectors

After the blockade had been lifted in May 1949, the Berliners were able to move around relatively freely, both inside the city and in the surrounding areas. This all changed in May 1952 when the government of the newly founded GDR gave the order to close most of the tram lines between West Berlin and its hinterland. The GDR inhabitants were no longer able to take their cars into the west sectors and West Berliners could not drive into the GDR. It was only possible to cross the sector border between West Berlin and the GDR on foot, by bicycle or by S-Bahn (urban railway). However the sector borders within the city, between East and West Berlin, continued to remain open. The closure measures were a reaction on the part of the GDR (and Moscow) to the signing of the German Treaty between the Federal Republic and the Western Allies on the 26th May 1952. This treaty granted the West German State extensive self determination rights and even paved the way for its membership in NATO. At the same time, the GDR government set a further boundary measure by cutting off all the telephone lines between East and West Berlin. In January 1953, the tram network, which up to this point had been operated jointly, was divided in two. From November 1952 West Berliners were officially prohibited from buying food and so-called industrial goods in East Berlin. Before then a large number of West Berliners had been taking advantage of the artificially low prices set by the GDR government for socialist political reasons.

Even at the height of the Cold War in and around Berlin, for example during the blockade in 1948–49, the three air corridors continued to remain untouched.

However, since the beginning of the 1950s there had been an increasing number of incidents, even in the air corridors. There was a particularly serious one on 29th April 1952, when an Air France passenger aircraft flying over Dessau was shot at by two Soviet Mig-15s. The aircraft was hit 89 times and five passengers sustained injuries. The pilot managed to steer the plane into the clouds and to land safely in Tempelhof shortly afterwards. The Western Powers lodged a strong protest against the attack which could easily have led to to a catastrophe. The Soviets repudiated this protest, maintaining that the Air France aircraft had strayed from the corridor and was therefore forced to land.

Barely a year later a much graver incident could easily have led to a direct confrontation between the East and West. On 12th March 1953, a British military aircraft on a flight from Berlin to Hamburg was shot at by Soviet interception aircraft and the seven members of the crew were killed. In this case, however, the Soviet commander-in-chief, Vasily I. Tschuikow, considered it appropriate to express his regret for this tragic incident.

Uprising against the SED regime

On 16th June 1953 about 200 construction workers from Stalinallee in East Berlin (today Karl-Marx-Allee) and from the building site at the Friedrichshain hospital, formed themselves into a protest march and marched to the "House of Ministries" *(Haus der Ministerien)* in Wilhelmstraße, the seat of the GDR government. On their way through the centre of Berlin more and more people joined in, so that the crowd was eventually over 4,000 strong. They chanted their demands for the raising of the work norms to be rescinded and the prices in state-owned shops *(HO-Läden)* to be lowered. They wanted their demands to be communicated to the Party Chairman, Ulbricht, in person. However, as neither Walter Ulbricht, nor Prime Minister,

Demonstrators burn the red flag that they have taken down from the Brandenburg Gate

Otto Grotewohl, made an appearance, the demonstrators dispersed without having achieved anything, chanting "We will return".

When they did indeed return the following morning, Wednesday 17th June, there were already 60,000 people laying siege to the government headquarters. This time they were not only demanding the withdrawal of the work norms, but also the resignation of the government and free elections. A central demand was the removal of the hated Ulbricht: "The goatee beard must go!" echoed through the streets. Within just a few hours, what had started as a worker's protest had turned into a full-blown revolutionary movement, whose aims were democracy and an end to the SED government and the division of Germany. Furthermore, the uprising was no longer confined to East Berlin but had spread throughout almost the whole of the GDR. On 17th June 1953 there were demonstrations in about 700 towns and communities and dozens of SED party offices and several prisons were besieged. A total of over a million people took to the streets all over the GDR demanding a better standard of living, freedom and democracy.

The SED government stood on the brink of defeat; a dejected Ulbricht thought that he had already been ousted and fled to the headquarters of the Soviet occupying power in Berlin-Karlshorst.

The rest of the world watched expectantly to see how the superpowers would react, because there was a possibility that the USA would support the rebellion against the GDR government and would then be able to force the Soviets to leave Berlin and East Germany. This would exactly corre-

East Berliners use stones to fight against the Soviet tanks on 17th June 1953

spond with the plans of the new Republican US Secretary of State, John Foster Dulles, who rejected the "containment" politics of the Democratic President, Harry S. Truman, and was passionately in favour of an offensive "roll back", which meant ousting the Soviet Union from the territory they were occupying. But would Moscow allow this to happen?

As the situation in East Berlin on 17th June 1953 intensified, Moscow sent in their tanks. At one o'clock a state of emergency was declared, all demonstrations were broken up by force of arms and numerous rebels were arrested. The rebellion against the GDR regime was also defeated by force in all the other centres of unrest, for example in Halle, Bitterfeld, Magdeburg, Leipzig, Dresden and Görlitz. Ulbricht and his comrades had only managed to remain in power on 17th June because of the military intervention by the Soviets; the majority

of the population had long grown tired of them. One of the tragedies of the 17th June uprising was that even the leadership in the Kremlin no longer agreed with Ulbricht's rigid methods and had already more or less decided to remove him. Paradoxically, or rather tragically, it was the attempt at rebellion against his repressive regime that actually saved Ulbricht from being removed from office because Moscow was no longer inclined to risk a change of State and Party leadership in view of the uncertain situation in the GDR.

The Western Allies protested against the bloody defeat of the people's rebellion in the GDR but they acted with restraint. They wanted to avoid a military confrontation with the Soviets in Berlin, as they had already managed to do in 1948, when the blockade was imposed. However, US President Eisenhower left it open as to whether this restraint would apply in all future situ-

Demonstrators on Potsdamer Platz seek cover from machine gun fire

ations. The time to get actively involved in the Eastern Bloc had not yet arrived.

Things could change and in fact, following the events of the "17th June", the USA strengthened its attempts to undermine the communist leadership in the Eastern Bloc countries. On the other hand the communist regime increased their repressive measures, which even certain "thaws", or phases of relaxation could not disguise.

The British Prime Minister, Winston Churchill, went even further in his restraint with the Soviets. Churchill granted the Soviet Union the right to take care of law and order behind closed doors inside their zone of occupation and to resort to military methods where necessary, as had already happened. "Were the Soviets simply supposed to stand and watch the east zone collapse into chaos and anarchy?"[11]

When assessing the defensive attitude of the Western powers in June 1953, one must consider that since 1950 a heated war had been raging between the East and the West in another region of the world – Korea. Here the conflict was between North Korea, supported by China and the Soviet Union, and the pro-west South Korea, supported mainly by the USA. In June 1953 the two sides in the Korean war were close to agreeing a cease-fire and this probably lessened America's desire to become involved in a conflict in Berlin and the GDR.

The people's rebellion of 17th June 1953 and its bloody defeat had resulted in the consolidation of the respective spheres of influence in Germany and the strengthening of the demarcation lines of the Cold War within Berlin.

The media

RIAS, the radio service in the American Sector, had played a fairly significant role in the events of 17th June, for example, by broadcasting to East Berlin and the whole of the GDR the main demands of the demonstrators. In general, the radio services and the press were important "weapons" in the Cold War fought in Berlin. At the same time it was much easier for the broadcasting stations in the West – especially RIAS and the US soldiers' radio station, AFN, and from 1960 increasingly television – to reach listeners or viewers in East Berlin and the GDR, than the other way round. Western pop music was in any case a much more attractive option than the sort of old-fashioned, stolid light music that characterised the music of the GDR stations until the 1980s – on the orders of the SED. For most young people in East Berlin, RIAS, German Radio (*Deutschlandfunk*) and AFN were a kind of "acoustic gateway to the world" through which they could get an idea of the western way of life – or what they thought it was.

To some extent RIAS and AFN actually contributed a bit on a daily basis to undermining the SED regime. In the GDR, a special youth radio station called DT64 had started up in 1964 and its mixture of modern music, including pop music from the West and some relatively snappy dialogue

Loudspeaker vans from the Berlin Senate intended to carry information and slogans to the other side of the Wall

RIAS reports on an outside broadcasting unit

soon made it very popular with young GDR listeners. With its unorthodox programme DT64, affiliated to Radio Berlin (Berliner Rundfunk), was mainly competing with RIAS and AFN for listeners in the GDR. In spite of repeated objections and reprimands from the SED leadership, in 1987 DT64 was able to become an independent station with its own frequency and continued broadcasting after the demise of the GDR. In 1993 it was changed into "Radio Sputnik".

GDR television was a more ambiguous area – on both sides of the Wall. The East German news and politically propagan-dist programmes, which were transmitted into people's homes from Berlin-Adlershof, attracted little interest. It was a different case with children's programmes and (old) feature films. These programmes actually had viewers on both sides of the Wall. Many people in the West enjoyed "The little Sandman" *(Sandmännchen)* and old Ufa filmstrips just as much as people in the East, even if a certain Karl-Eduard von Schnitzler in on "the black channel" vented his spleen against the "class enemy" in the west. One could always turn the television off.

A playground for spies

Of course, the second oldest profession in the world always stood in a prominent position on the frontline of the Cold War. Spies and agents in Berlin had especially favourable working conditions because until the Wall was built in 1961 it was relatively easy to move around between the East and the West, particularly for members of the Occupying Powers.

Berlin quickly became a real playground for the secret services on both sides of the Cold War. There was nowhere else where they could gather information at such close quarters to their opponents and start operations against the other side. As a CIA agent once described it: "If the Soviet Military Commander in Bucharest or Warsaw telephoned Moscow, the call went via Berlin."[12] The secret services were naturally present in large numbers.

On 4th July 1945, the very first day that they had access to Berlin after it had fallen to the Soviets, the Americans had had a group of secret service personnel flown into the city. At this point in time the construction of a Soviet secret service was already in full swing. The Berlin headquarters of the KGB was in Berlin-Karlshorst, in the building of the former St. Antonius hospital.

By the beginning of the 1950s there were about 800 secret service employees working there. After the people's rebellion of 17th June 1953 this number was significantly increased. The CIA was based in the residential suburb of Dahlem at 19–21 Föhrenweg. MI6, the British Secret Service, resided on the Reichssportfeld in buildings which had been built as part of the complex for the Olympic Games in 1936.

Only Vienna, which since 1945 had also been a four sector city, could also lay claim to such a high concentration of spies at that time as the former Reich capital, Berlin. In the 1950s there were about 80 secret service authorities active in Berlin. They attempted to camouflage themselves behind various façades, ranging from jam factories to research institutes.[13]

Both sides stopped at nothing in this war of spies. In the 1950s, in particular, there were countless undercover operations, including spying on the enemy, military and economic espionage and kidnapping, the latter being a special favourite of the Soviets and their helpers in the GDR

One of the men suspected of espionage is brought before the American military court

Ministry for State Security. The US CIA and other anti-communist groups were also not always selective in the methods they used to try and inflict damage on the Soviets and the SED regime.

The espionage tunnel

The espionage tunnel under the sector border, which was to be one of the most costly and above all the most productive operations mounted by the American and British secret services in Berlin, actually turned out to be a relative disgrace.

On 24th April 1956 the Soviets held an outdoor press conference where they presented a 600 metre tunnel which had been dug from the West into the eastern borough of Treptow and which was equipped with the most modern bugging devices. The CIA and the British SIS (Secret Intelligence Service) had apparently been tapping the East Berlin telephone network there and bugging the conversations and telegrams of the Soviet military in a big way.

A Soviet Officer vociferously gave vent to his indignation and explained to the clearly impressed journalists that the tunnel had been accidentally discovered during maintenance works on the telephone network.

However, this was not the case at all. The Soviets had actually known about the bugged tunnel down to the last detail because the British double agent, George Blake, had already told them about it in the planning stages and had always kept them informed about its further progress.[14]

The work on the tunnel had begun in the spring of 1954. First of all, for camouflage purposes, the Americans erected an alleged US Army warehouse directly on the sector border. From there the five metre deep tunnel was dug eastwards. During its construction US agents were

practising on a dummy tunnel of similar construction in New Mexico. In May 1955 the original in Berlin was ready for use.

The Soviets were now faced with a dilemma. Should they have the tunnel busted before the bugging began? This would have meant placing double agent Blake, their source in the SIS, at considerable risk. The decision was made in Moscow to protect their source and let their opponents carry on, until the most harmless opportunity of "discovering" the tunnel presented itself. Moreover, the Soviets could now have even used their knowledge about the tunnel for the purpose of misinforming the enemy. However, it seems that for whatever reason, they chose not to make use of this opportunity. Having discovered that the Western Powers were bugging them, they simply increased internal security measures with regard to telephone conversations (codes, encoding etc.). That meant that about 500,000 reels of tape onto which the CIA and the SIS had recorded roughly 443,000 individual conversations did not only contain "rubbish" or rather verbal fog transmitted from Karlshorst. The operation is meant to have provided the West with much more important information, such as details of the growing atomic power of the Soviet airforce in Poland and the GDR. To this extent the whole operation was somewhat of a disgrace for the West, but not entirely fruitless.

The kidnapping of political opponents

Secret services are not squeamish and the KGB and the Stasi (the GDR state security service) in particular, often resorted to kidnapping as a means of catching people they didn't like. This was especially easy for them in Berlin where the sector border was open until 1961.

Soviet soldiers and a GDR policeman (Volkspolizist) show the espionage tunnel to the press

One of the most spectacular cases was the kidnapping of Walter Linse, an anti-communist activist. Suspecting nothing, he left his flat in the Lichterfelde district of Berlin on 8th July 1952, Suddenly he was pulled into a car disguised as a taxi and driven over the sector border into East Berlin. The KGB and the Stasi had hired four professional criminals for the kidnapping, who each received 1,000 marks for their work.

The 49 year old had come to the attention of the secret services in the East because he was one of the leading activists of the "investigation branch of liberal lawyers" (UfJ). This organisation, founded in 1949 and based in Berlin, had made it its job to document legal injustice in the GDR and to give legal advice to GDR citizens, for example when they were visiting West Berlin. The UfJ had set up a network of informers in the GDR to help them achieve their aims and were financed in the main by the CIA, which from 1951/52 was pressing for this network to prepare for para-military deployment.[15] Linse's kidnapping was followed by the arrest of several dozen of his connections and informers for the "liberal lawyers".

Two later days later, at a rally in West Berlin, Ernst Reuter addressed a crowd of over 25,000 and protested in the strongest terms against these abductions. After months of interrogations, first in the Stasi prison at Hohenschönhausen and then in a Soviet secret service prison in Berlin Karlshorst, Walter von Linse was sentenced to death by a military tribunal and in December 1953 he was shot in a Moscow prison.

Another kidnapping victim – Heinz Brandt – was at first very sympathetic towards the construction of socialism and had even been actively involved as an SED official in 1945. However, as a communist resistance worker against the Nazis, he had spent years in a concentration camp and the violent defeat of the people's rebellion of 17th June 1953 made him start to have doubts about the SED regime. In 1956 Heinz Brandt finally broke his allegiance to communism when the full extent of Stalin's crimes became known and in 1958 he fled to the West and worked as a trade union journalist committed to liberal-democratic socialism. The KGB and the Stasi pursued renegades with especial hatred and on 16th June 1961 Heinz Brandt was lured into a trap in West Berlin. While he was out on a date with a woman, his whisky was spiked and shortly afterwards he collapsed unconscious on the street. A Stasi detachment bundled Brandt into a car and abducted him across the open border into East Berlin. Following a secret trial Brandt was sentenced in 1962 by the highest court in the GDR to 13 years' imprisonment for alleged spying.

In his case continuous protests by the West finally bore fruit, not least because of the involvement of the recently founded aid organisation, Amnesty International. After three years behind bars Heinz Brandt was released from the GDR prison and deported to the West.

A further kidnapping case which caused a sensation was possibly not one at all. At least, the Federal German judges did not believe there had been an kidnapping when they sentenced Otto John, the former head of the Bonn office for the defence of the constitution (*Verfassungsgericht*), to four years imprisonment for offences against the Official Secrets Act. All the assertions made by the accused that he had been abducted by the Stasi, taken to East Berlin and forced into the making incriminating statements fell on deaf ears and even large sections of the West German public thought that John was a traitor.

Abduction or high treason? To this day the "John case", one of the biggest political scandals in the Federal Republic, has not been unequivocally explained.

This much is certain: late in the evening, on 20th July 1954, Otto John, who was 45 years old at the time, drove over the sector border into East Berlin with his friend, a doctor named Wolfgang Wohlgemut. The critical question is whether he was drugged beforehand by Wohlgemut on the instructions of the Stasi or changed sides of his own free will.

It has to be said that John did not look much like a kidnapping victim when he held a press conference in East Berlin at which he strongly criticised the conditions in West Germany. He denounced in particular the growing influence of ex-Nazi sympathisers or perpetrators in West German politics and criticised Adenauer's re-armament plans. In the months that followed he repeated these accusations on various occasions and the GDR press made propaganda capital out of them. It was actually true that Otto John, who had been involved in the preparations for the assassination attempt on Hitler in 1944 and subsequently fled to Great Britain when it failed, had shown increasing concern at the return of ex-Nazi sympathisers and perpetrators to key positions in the Federal Republic. To this extent he was only speaking out publicly in the GDR about what he actually thought. Whether this also includes his repeated assertion that he considered the GDR to be the better German state has to be left as an open question.

Just as spectacular – and veiled in mystery – as his move to East Berlin was Otto John's return to the West, when he simply registered at a West Berlin police

An anti-Stalinist balloon campaign mounted by the "task force against inhumanity"

station on 12th December 1955. He stated
that he had used a lecture at the Humboldt
University to shake off his Stasi guards
to flee to the west, hidden in a Danish
journalist's car. In the weeks that followed
John never tired of explaining that he
was a victim of a kidnapping and that his
appearances in East Berlin and the GDR
were all acts of self-protection and only
tactical manoeuvres.

However neither the majority of the
West Germans nor the judges at the Federal court believed his version of events.
They aligned themselves with Reinhard
Gehlen, head of BND, the West German
news service and one of those Nazi sympathisers whose advancement had sickened
John so much, when he said, "once a traitor, always a traitor!"

By this, Gehlen meant to belittle John's
resistance to the Nazi regime and his
statements in the trial against the former
Wehrmacht Field Marshal Erich von
Manstein as well as John's critical attitude towards certain developments in the
Federal Republic.

Since numerous public archives were
opened in 1989, it seems certain that the
summing up by a former KGB officer fits
the "John case" best. He said that John
"came of his own free will but was not
willing to stay".[16] In fact, there is much to
suggest that Otto John went on his own
initiative to talk with political leaders in
Moscow and East Berlin about alternatives
to the course being taken by the Adenauer
government. He seemed for a time to accept that his stay in the GDR would be
used for propaganda purposes by the SED.
However, both the ideological dogmatism
he encountered and the depressing conditions in the GDR soon seemed to have
convinced him of the hopelessness of his
undertaking. His return to the West was
the logical consequence. The fact that in
the Federal Republic he was then mainly

viewed as a traitor, or at least a dubious
character, and not as a resistance fighter
or as someone sending a critical warning,
is part of the tragedy of Otto John's story,
which is a very German story.

The task force against inhumanity

If the SED controlled press kept pub-
lishing reports of western agents and
saboteurs who were "stirring things up"
against the GDR, this mainly served as
a cheap explanation for the economic
problems and lack of provisions in the
GDR and as a justification for more severe
repressions. The true reasons for the mis-
management of the economy and suppression had to be kept hidden even if they had
their roots in the Stalinist system.

However these tales of espionage were
not complete fantasy as there were definitely groups, mainly of young people, who
were working with great zeal to plot the fall
of the SED regime.

The "task force against inhumanity"
is one example. The KgU (*Kampfgruppe
gegen Unmenschlichkeit*) was founded
in West Berlin in 1948 by Rainer Hilde-
brandt, an idealistic firebrand who in 1944
had contacts with the military resistance
against the Nazi regime. At the beginning
of the sixties he was responsible for the
construction of the Berlin Wall museum,
the "Haus am Checkpoint Charlie". At
first, the group was mainly concerned
with looking after released prisoners, as
well as documenting the acts of injustice
committed by the legal system in the GDR.
They also collected data on the economic,
political and military situation in the GDR
which was gleaned from an extensive network of informers. The group, which was
partly financed by the CIA, became more
radical from 1951 onwards and distributed
pamphlets by means of air balloons for

Exchanging agents on the Glienicker Bridge on 12th February 1986

instance, and organised targeted sabotage and disruptive actions. In 1952/53 they succeeded in disrupting production by faking instructions and orders for goods, they diverted goods trains and managed to heavily restrict any contacts that GDR companies had abroad.

The GDR reacted with extreme harshness. In 1952 alone, 200 KgU members and associates were arrested and given draconian sentences. In 1955 two "task force" contacts in Weimar who had supplied military information were sentenced to death and executed.

In October 1951, 18 senior pupils from Werdau in Saxony, who had among other things distributed leaflets for the KgU,

were given long prison sentences. All these arrests led to the KgU increasingly being publicly accused in the West of a lack of professionalism and carelessness. From 1953 onwards the group stopped undertaking any operations which were too risky and in 1959 the "task force against inhumanity" was disbanded.

Exchanging secret agents

The Glienicke Bridge, idyllically situated between Potsdam and Berlin-Zehlendorf. A misty November evening, dimly lit by a few lanterns, not a soul or vehicle to be seen for miles around. Suddenly some cars with darkened windows drive on to the bridge. From the other side of the bridge military vehicles approach and move towards them. The cars are now face to face. Some men get out and walk towards each other. This is the way many of the post-war spy thrillers depicted the scene and indeed several secret agents were exchanged on this bridge.

Many small fry were amongst them, but also one or two big ones like US pilot, Gary Powers, who was shot down over the Soviet Union in his U2 spy plane in 1960. In October 1962 the Americans released the Soviet "master spy" Rudolf I. Abel, who had been working in atomic espionage in the USA, in exchange for Powers.

The most extensive operation on the Glienicke Bridge took place on 12th June 1985 when a total of 27 people were exchanged. 23 "busted " agents and associates of the CIA, who had been working in Poland and the GDR, crossed sides with four Eastern Bloc agents who had fallen into the hands of the CIA.

This process of exchanging agents mostly went on quietly and secretly and was only made public after the event. In February 1986, however, the international press got wind of plans for a spectacular spy exchange and for several days crowds of them besieged the western side of the bridge. On 11th February 1986, after spending years in a prison camp, the Soviet dissident Anatoly Schtscharanski walked to freedom across the Glienicker Bridge and was picked up by car by the US Ambassador of the day. In exchange for Schtscharanski, the West released eight eastern agents who crossed the bridge into the East.

Paradoxically, this bridge between Potsdam and West Berlin, the middle of which formed the border between East and West and the front line of the Cold War, was called the "Bridge of Unity". This was the name given to it by the GDR government in 1949 and it was not changed until after reunification.

Co-operation between the Allies

Among all the conflicts there were also some areas of life in Berlin in which the four victorious allies worked together relatively harmoniously; these were in Air Safety Control and in the administration of Spandau Prison.

After the Allied Control Council had disintegrated and the Soviets had withdrawn from the Allied Kommandantura in 1948, these were the only two institutions where the four Allies were still working together. The Berlin Air Safety Centre was established in February 1946 to guarantee the safe handling of flights to and from Berlin. It was responsible for a total area of 3,200 square metres, of which 2,320 square metres were outside Berlin and was housed in a wing of the Allied Control Council building in Schöneberg (in the American Sector). From 1949 onwards the technical department of the Air Safety Centre was accommodated in Tempelhof Airport.

The four powers knew about every single air movement and ensured a safe route for each one. In disputed cases there was a special "confrontation room" available but this seldom had to be used. The Soviets and the Western Allies worked constructively together in the Air Safety Control Centre right up to the fall of the Wall and the reunification of Berlin, even during the blockade and the Airlift.

The "Allied War Crimes Prison" had been set up by the four victorious allies in October 1946 in the Spandau fortress prison, a brick building dating from the year 1881.

The only inmates were the seven main war criminals who had been given custodial sentences at the Nuremberg military

Guards from the Spandau War Criminals Prison returning after the changing of guard

The Berlin Air Safety Centre in the Allied Control Council building

trials were housed here. This included Rudolf Hess, once the "Deputy Führer", the former Armaments Minister, Albert Speer and the former head of the German navy, Karl Dönitz.

Each of the four victorious allies provided the prison guards for a month at a time and the prison was run by four equal ranking Commandants who also had monthly tours of duty. After Albert Speer was released in 1966, Rudolf Hess was the only remaining inmate and when he committed suicide in August 1987, Spandau Prison was demolished.

The Battle for Cultural Supremacy

The Cold War was not always fought with the gloves off, as it was during the blockades, tank duels and kidnappings. Particularly in Berlin, where the borders remained open until 1961, the East-West conflict was fought in the form of a comparatively peaceful "battle of systems", which was all about which side had the better social model.

The "battlefields" for this "soft" system rivalry were, for example, in housing, town planning, culture and art, consumer goods and not least social politics. As the Soviet Party leader, Khrushchev, stated so clearly in 1956, "There (in Berlin *T.F.*) not only an ideological battle is being fought, but also an economic battle between socialism and capitalism. The comparison is being made to see which system is creating the better material conditions …"[17]

This weapon-free battle has left numerous traces in the city – some of them really positive – which can still be seen today. These include the blocks of flats on the former Stalinallee in the borough of "Mitte" (today Karl-Marx-Allee), the Hansa district in the west and the relatively large number of theatres and opera houses.

Prestige projects from the drawing board

At the beginning of the 1950s the "Stalinallee" project in the boroughs of Mitte and Friedrichshain demonstrated the SED's concept of a "socialist city" and "socialist housing". The plans for the blocks of flats and shops along the 2.5 kilometre long avenue connecting Alexanderplatz and Frankfurter Tor were drawn up by a collective of architects led by Hermann Henselmann and construction started in 1952. These buildings, consisting of up to nine floors, contained a total of 2,200 apartments, with mostly two or three bedrooms and at ground level there were numerous shops and restaurants. The style was strongly orientated towards the Soviet "wedding cake style" model and they were fitted out with a bathroom, a district heating system and part parquet flooring. The building construction and materials were of an extremely high standard so that the "Stalinallee" soon became a most desirable area to live.

The grand avenue (*Magistrale*), in places widened to 125 metres, was repeatedly used for military parades and mass processions.

It was as if the "Hansa district" *(Hansaviertel)* in West Berlin, erected within the context of the International Building Exhibition (IBA) in 1957, was an alternative draft to the Stalinallee, the "first socialist street of the GDR". Financed mainly with funds from the social housing budget, 48 individual high-rise buildings containing a total of 1,300 apartments were built on an area on the edge of the Tiergarten. Before the Second World Was this had been a middle-class residential area with some quite palatial housing which in 1943 had been almost completely destroyed in bombing raids. The Hansa district stood out because of its free development and its extensive lawns. The designs for the individual buildings came from the most renowned modern architects of the day, including Alvar Aalto, Walter Gropius, Le Corbusier and Oscar Niemeyer. The fact that so many architects took part in the project meant that the overall impression of the Hansa district was one of rich variety.

Stalinallee in 1954 (today Karl-Marx-Allee)

A direct comparison between two other large city building projects was no longer as easy as it had been between Stalinallee and the Hansa District after the Berlin Wall divided the city.

As a result of the destruction inflicted by the war, even in the 1960s and 1970s both halves of the city were faced with the task of creating affordable housing on a massive scale.

In West Berlin the answer to this structural and social problem was provided by the "Märkisches Viertel" and the "Gropiusstadt", two spectacular, if controversial, large housing estates, each with 17,000 apartments housing a total of almost 60,000 people.

They initially attracted only praise from residents and town planners because of the combination of good quality accommodation at a reasonable price but then in the eighties the Märkisches Viertel in particu-lar fell into disrepute as an anonymous "housing machine" and a hive of social problems.

In East Berlin everything was on an even larger scale. Erich Honecker, who had taken over from Walter Ulbricht as Party leader and head of state in 1971, had de-clared "the solution to the housing problem up to 1990" as one of his central policies. In fact the provision of cheap housing for the people was to serve as a central legiti-misation argument for GDR socialism in general and the power politics of the SED in particular.

In 1976, not just a large housing estate but the whole new city district of Marzahn was created on the sandy soil of East Berlin. In just fifteen months, dozens of concrete slab complexes were built incorporating a total of 62,000 apartments, numerous shops, child day care centres, schools and leisure facilities. Transport links consist-

View from one of the tower blocks in the Hansa District (Hansaviertel)

ing of a new system and a special S-Bahn (urban railway) line were also constructed. The sheer size and architectural uniformity of Marzahn seemed rather repulsive to visitors, but for many East Berlin families it fulfilled the long cherished wish for a modern apartment with a bathroom, central heating and other amenities.

This meant that for a long time Marzahn was also a really desirable residential area, until social problems and tensions increased in the aftermath of the economic and social decline which followed the collapse of the SED regime and the reunification of Berlin.

Overall one could state, somewhat cynically, that the grand projects of the seventies and eighties, like the Märkisches Viertel in the West and Marzahn in the East, were not so different from each other as the prestige projects of Stalinallee and Hansa-Viertel had been in their time.

Subsidies and flourishing cultures

One of the especially positive sides of the system rivalry in divided Berlin was the rich cultural life that both East and West Berlin were prepared to spend money on. This was because theatre and opera were supposed to contribute to the higher standing of each of their respective systems. The culturally minded of the whole city benefited from this rivalry, because until the Wall was built in 1961, they were able to enjoy top class productions, especially in the theatres and opera houses. All they needed was an S-Bahn ticket.

In the first years of the Cold War the East had the edge in this competition. This was partly due to the fact that most of the traditional theatres like the Deutsches Theater and the Theater am Schiffbauerdamm were in the Soviet Sector, but the

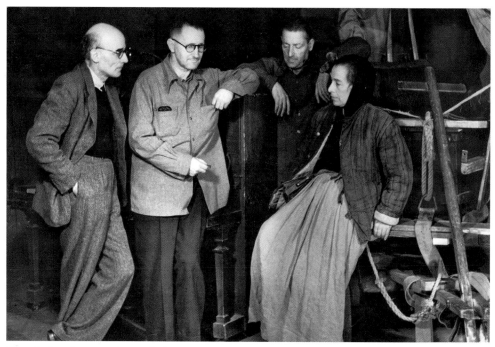

Bertolt Brecht at a rehearsal of "Mother Courage" in the Deutsches Theater, East Berlin

performing arts also flourished because the Soviet Occupying Power promoted them.

In the 1950s, Wolfgang Langhoff's productions at the Deutsches Theater in Schumannstraße or Bertolt Brecht's performances of his own plays (from 1953 in the Berliner Ensemble on the Schiffbauerdamm) received particular international acclaim. On the operatic stage, it was Walter Feinstein's productions at the East Berlin Komische Oper, with their strong realism, which enjoyed a high international reputation.

West Berlin responded to the challenge. In 1951 the Schillertheater was opened on Bismarckstraße and with Boleslaw Barlog as Director, it enjoyed considerable success until the late 1960s, with many highly regarded productions of classics, as well as plays by contemporary authors, such as Samuel Beckett.

After the Berlin Wall went up, it was no longer possible to make a direct comparison between the two very lively worlds of theatre and this "fertile" chapter of the Cold War, when cultural rivalry in Berlin actually helped business, came to an abrupt end. In the 1970s in West Berlin the new generation, for example Peter Stein who founded the "Schaubühne", gave fresh impetus to the world of theatre and were received with considerable enthusiasm.

In East Berlin the innovative creative force of the post-war years gave way to a gradual "stultification" in the world of theatre and opera, caused to a large extent by the increasing influence of the SED cultural bureaucracy.

Nevertheless, a number of people still managed even in the 1970s and 1980s to create some space of their own where artistic originality could flourish, for example the operatic productions by Ruth Berghaus

Advertising poster for the World Festival of Youth in 1951

and Harry Kupfer and the plays of a certain Heiner Müller.

However, it wasn't only in the arts where a lot of money was spent in Cold War Berlin. Because of the political circumstances, both halves of the city were in some respects granted privileges not enjoyed by other towns and regions. East Berlin, for example, was always given preferential treatment in the provision of food and consumer goods.

On the other side of the Wall, for decades half the West Berlin budget was paid for out of Federal finances and in addition, every employee in West Berlin enjoyed an 8 per cent "Berlin allowance" in their monthly pay packet.

On the other hand, these subsidies were not just "gifts" but really necessary compensation measures to mitigate the economic consequences of division. After 1948 numerous industrial firms had left Berlin because of the uncertain political and economic situation and this had cost tens of thousands of jobs. The long, and until the 1972 Four Power Agreement, insecure access routes to and from West Berlin made the transport of goods both difficult and costly. Financial support and subsidies were essential to prevent the collapse of the West Berlin economy. However, the fact that these subsidies created a certain "dependence" mentality among the West Berliners, whether they were workers, employers, teachers or members of the city council,

and attracted crooks and subsidy cheats, is another story.

Inviting the world to Berlin

After twelve years of Nazi rule and the devastation resulting from the war, Berliners in both halves of the city began to long for a little cosmopolitan flair. In 1951 the International Film Festival started to bring back some sparkle and glamour to West Berlin. In just a few years, alongside Cannes and Venice, it became one of the three most important film festivals and every year in June it attracted lots of stars and starlets to the city. Until the Wall was built in 1961, East Berliners could also watch most of these new films – provided they could get hold of a ticket – and get a taste of the big wide world.

From time to time, even the SED regime invited foreigners into East Berlin, although this preferably took the form of strictly organised mass events. Twice, in 1951 and 1973, the "World Festival of Youth and Students" took place; mammoth events which on each occasion involved the participation of several hundred thousand young people from the GDR and tens of thousand guests from all over the world.

There were of course the inevitable parades and rallies, but most of the participants used the "Festival" to meet up informally with young people of the same age from home and abroad.

At the Film festival in 1952 "Astronauts" advertise the film "End Station Moon"
(Endstation Mond)

The Khrushchev Ultimatum

After the suppression of the uprising on 17th June 1953, for several years relative peace reigned in the "frontline city" of Berlin. For a while, the Cold War was waged elsewhere: in Vietnam, where in French colonial troops had suffered a devastating defeat at the hands of the Vietminh, the Communist Liberation Front, supported by Moscow and China, and in Hungary, where in November 1956 Soviet tanks had rolled in to put down an people's uprising against the Stalinist regime. Similarly in November 1956, the British and French had failed in their attempt to use military force to recapture the Suez Canal which had been put under Egyptian state control. All these conflicts were part of the global battle between the East and the West for power and spheres of influence.

In November 1958, Berlin once again dramatically became the focus of attention in the Cold War. In the so-called Khrushchev Ultimatum of 27th November 1958 Moscow demanded nothing less than the total withdrawal of Western Allied troops from Berlin. The three west sectors were to be "demilitarised" and turned into a "Free City of Berlin". The actual text read: "The ... most correct solution would be the reunification of the western part of Berlin ... with the eastern part, whereby Berlin would be a united city belonging to the country where it lies" – namely the GDR.[18] However, Khrushchev himself admitted that at this point in time such a huge demand was a total illusion. "Basically, the USA, Great Britain and France are only interested in West Berlin because they are used this "frontline city" ... as a deployment zone for enemy activity against the socialist states ... The ending of the illegal

occupation of West Berlin would not inflict any damage on the USA, Great Britain or France; on the contrary, it would considerably improve the international atmosphere."[19]

Moscow was thus making a direct grab for Berlin and this instantly intensified the confrontation with the Western Powers. If the USA and their allies did not meet the Soviets' demands within six months, Khrushchev threatened to sign a separate peace treaty with the GDR handing over full "sovereignty over land, water and air".[20] This alarmed the West because it would mean that if tensions increased, Ulbricht and his comrades would be able to declare a blockade against West Berlin which could even include closing the air corridors. However, it was now out of the question for the Western Allies to back down in Berlin, even if the Soviet Foreign Secretary was openly threatening war when he declared in a speech on 22nd December 1958 that Berlin could become a "second Sarajevo", by triggering another world war. He was referring to the Bosnian city of Sarajavo where in June 1914 Franz Ferdinand, the heir to the Austrian throne, was murdered, which indirectly led to the outbreak of the First World War (whose origins were of course much more complex than the assassination of a relative of the Austrian Kaiser).

A war of nerves began which lasted for several weeks and the French President, de Gaulle, was certainly not far off the mark when at the beginning of 1958 he spoke to Chancellor Konrad Adenauer of the "the most dangerous situation since the end of war". In fact, in the capital cities of the West the possibility of an exchange of atomic weapons was not excluded. When asked to do so by the Americans, the West

Nikita Krushchev on a visit to Berlin on 19th May 1960

German Defence Minister at the time, Franz Josef Strauß, named a military exercise area in the GDR as a possible target for an atomic bomb. This would signal a "final warning" before the big atomic attack against the Soviet Union",[21] because the Western politicians were convinced that everything depended on demonstrating toughness and determination to the Soviet Union.[22] However, much to the annoyance of the USA and the other allies, this stance was often lacking in the British government under the Conservative leadership of Prime Minister Harold Macmillan.

The British Government considered granting far-reaching concessions to the Soviet Union, for example a *de facto* recognition of the GDR which the other Western Powers strongly disapproved of. Macmillan also doubted the willingness of many of his compatriots to fights a war on behalf of West Berlin as this would mean fighting for "the freedom of a people who had tried twice in this century to destroy us (Great Britain)".[23] If London wanted to grant concessions to the Soviet Union, the governments in Washington and Paris showed even greater toughness, strengthened by urgent appeals from Bonn, not to back down one iota from the positions in Berlin.

On the other hand, during these months, the world witnessed a Khrushchev who was bursting with self-confidence and who proclaimed that the Soviet Union and its allies would "overtake" the West in the foreseeable future. In fact the Soviet Union had recently notched up some successes which had not gone unnoticed in the West, especially in October 1957 with the launch of "Sputnik", the first man-made satellite. Even the rate of growth of the Soviet economy at the end of the 1950s seem to justify the Kremlin's optimism to a certain extent. Even if it was objectively outside that realms of reality that the Soviet Union would "overtake the West" – in 1960 the economic situation in the Soviet Union and the other Eastern Bloc countries had in part dramatically deteriorated – the Soviet Union was certainly still a opponent who had to be reckoned with, especially militarily and in matters of weapon technology.[24]

Then 27th May 1959 arrived and the ultimatum passed without anything happening. On the contrary, the Four Powers had started up negotiations again and in mid-May 1959 a conference of Foreign Ministers was called in Geneva. However, despite several months of talks on questions affecting central Berlin and Germany, there was no rapprochement, although at least there no more mention of the Soviet Union's "ultimatum". Without saying a word, as it were, both sides had come to an agreement that the problem of "West Berlin" should be de-dramatised.

Until the next confrontation – which was to follow quite shortly.

The Berlin Wall

The building of the Wall

Berlin in the 1950s was an "open city" in the sense that, despite the political division, it was possible to move around between the four sectors relatively easily. It was not only the 3.5 million Berliners who benefited from this situation – especially the West Berliners who worked in East Berlin (of whom there were over 50,000) and could go to the theatre and buy cheap groceries there and East Berliners who were able to watch the latest Hollywood films in the western part of the city. Many GDR citizens, too, used the special status of Berlin to finally turn their backs on "The Workers' and Farmers' State". The inner German border had been sealed since May 1952 but getting to Berlin was no problem at all. Having arrived in East Berlin, one only had to take the S-Bahn to get into West Berlin. Year after year, over 150,000 GDR citizens used this loophole to flee to the West. All that was necessary was the purchase of an S-Bahn ticket – and a little bit of caution, because the GDR People's Police *(Volkspolizei)* were more thorough with their checks on the access routes to East Berlin. Whole families with a lot of luggage aroused suspicion, so people just took essentials so that it looked as if they were out for the day. This mass exodus to the West, which politicians in the West like to describe as people "voting

The building of the Wall in August 1961 near Friedrichstraße

with their feet", became more and more of a problem for the GDR. The refugees, who were mainly young and well-qualified, were needed in industry, hospitals and universities. Between 1945 and the end of 1960 over 2.5 million people had fled to the West, so that there was a real threat that the GDR could eventually be bled dry.[25] Among themselves the SED leadership began to talk fairly openly about the causes for the mass exodus. For example, at the start of 1961, Ulbricht bluntly announced in the Politbüro that in over 60 per cent of cases people were leaving the GDR "due to (mainly) economic reasons (associated) with shortcomings in the workplace."[26]

However, all this internal self-criticism did not deter Ulbricht from devising radical measures.

Even the Soviet leaders in the Kremlin and the governments in the West were aware that the flood of refugees meant that the SED regime was heading for a crisis that threatened its very existence. In February 1961 the situation in and around Berlin dramatically intensified. It was here, on the open border between two enemy power blocks, that the future of the GDR was decided.

At a conference in Moscow in March 1961, Walter Ulbricht suggested halting the flood of refugees with "a barbed wire fence". This was vetoed by Khrushchev who stated that, "a total sealing off" was not part of the "current Soviet tactics", but Ulbricht did not give up and continued pursuing his aim to stop the mass exodus from the GDR.

In the meantime a summit meeting between Nikita Khrushchev and President John F. Kennedy had been set up in Vienna. Once again the topic for discussion was Berlin, the eternal bone of contention in the Cold War. However, instead of détente, the summit brought a dramatic heightening of tension. Khrushchev

persisted in his well-known demands; the withdrawal of the Allies from Berlin and the creation of a "free city of West Berlin" without any internationally recognised ties with the Federal Republic. These demands were completely unacceptable to Kennedy, who had been hit hard by the Bay of Pigs disaster in April 1961, the failed attempt by exiled Cubans, supported by the CIA, to overthrow Fidel Castro. The atmosphere in the discussions between the two most powerful men in the world became increasingly frosty. Both of them openly threatened war. Khrushchev's words were: "I would like peace, but if you want war than that's your business. Kennedy's reply was: "Then it will be a cold winter."[27] Kennedy's depression, which was testified to many times after this conversation, proves that they were both serious. Khrushchev on the other hand seemed to fail to recognise Kennedy's determination in this dangerous game. One of his close associates later said: "Kennedy believed that Khrushchev could use atomic weapons – a mistake. Khrushchev thought that Kennedy was too soft to use atomic weapons – another mistake. Both of them had miscalculated. It was only by chance that the world got away with it."[28]

On 25th July 1961 President Kennedy made a speech on television in which he clearly spelt out the American position. "We have given our word that we regard an attack upon Berlin as an attack upon us all. We cannot and will not permit the Communists to drive us out of Berlin. ...We do not want to fight, but we have fought before."[29] This was the first time that Kennedy had spoken so clearly about the danger of a war. Khrushchev also demonstrated greater determination than ever. He told John McCloy, the American High Commissioner in the Federal Republic, that Kennedy's television address was a "declaration of war, an ultimatum." He

The Wall at Potsdamer Platz in November 1961

was to inform Kennedy that, "we accept his ultimatum ... We will not start the war, but we will not shrink back from it if it is forced upon us."[30] Berlin lay under the shadow of an atomic war.

During those tense weeks, it must have struck observant onlookers how often the US government included in their declarations on Berlin three so-called "essentials" which they would defend at any cost: 1. Western military presence in Berlin, 2. free access to Berlin and 3. freedom of movement in West Berlin. There was no mention of East Berlin. At the end of July Kennedy stated even more clearly to his closest advisors: "I can hold the alliance together (NATO. T.F.) in order to defend West Berlin, but not to keep access to East Berlin open."[31]

Six weeks previously Ulbricht had held a thought-provoking press conference in

East Berlin. To the question from a West German journalist as to whether a "free city of West Berlin" would mean that the state border would then run along the Brandenburg Gate, the SED leader replied: "I understand your question to meant that there are people in the Federal Republic who would like us to mobilise the construction workers in our capital to erect a wall. ... No-one has the intention of erecting a wall."

In the meantime, less than two weeks later, Ulbricht met the Soviet Ambassador in East Berlin and once again described to him the precarious situation in the GDR. "The growing flood of refugees is affecting every aspect of life in the Republic. Things will soon explode. (The Ambassador) should inform Khrushchev that if the current situation of an open border continues to operate, a collapse is inevitable."[32]

This dramatic appeal had its desired effect in Moscow. At the beginning of August 1961 the Kremlin leadership gave its agreement and Ulbricht was given a free hand to seal the border.

Shortly after midnight on 13th August 1961, a Sunday, West Berlin was sealed off. GDR Border Police rolled out barbed wire along the sector border and the border with the GDR hinterland. They ripped up the road surfaces and drove concrete posts into the ground. All the underground and S-Bahn lines running between the two halves of the city were cut off. The "Berlin loophole" had been closed. Two days later troops of construction workers began to build a wall through the middle of the city.

People around the world watched as if spellbound. Would the West accept the violent division of the city or would they force the removal of the barriers, possibly with military means? Yet again the question in Berlin was, "war or peace?".

A West Berlin policeman recalls the dramatic moments at the Brandenburg Gate on that fateful 13th August 1961: "At first we thought that the (GDR Border Police) were going to overrun us and march into West Berlin, but they remained on the precise centimetre of the sector border." That was the decisive point: the Border Police stopped at the border. As President Kennedy had said: "I can hold the alliance together (NATO. T.F.) in order to defend West Berlin, but not to keep access to East Berlin open." That meant that as long as the barriers remained restricted to East Berlin, the Western Alliance would keep quiet. In fact, it was indeed the case that the building of the wall had not infringed those "three essentials" that Kennedy wanted to defend at any cost: free access to West Berlin for the Western Allies, the presence of the West in Berlin and self-determination for the West Berliners. There were, of course, strong protests by the Western governments about the closing of the border, but there were no concrete countermeasures to keep open that "loophole into freedom" between East and West Berlin. To his closest advisers Kennedy even seemed relieved about developments: "Khrushchev would not have had a wall built if he really wanted West Berlin … it's not a pleasant solution but a wall is a damned sight better than a war."[33]

Here was no lack of political irony. What most of the world saw as the problem, the erection of a wall through the middle of Berlin on the front-line of the Cold War, was for Kennedy the solution to the problem. Moscow and East Berlin had brutally stopped the flood of refugees and at the same time had refrained from attempting any access to West Berlin. The building of the Wall was thus not the beginning of a new Berlin crisis but the end of the crisis. In Paris and London people seemed to take a similar view and acted accordingly. French President De Gaulle continued his leave in the capital whilst the British Prime Minister Macmillan did not allow his shoot in Scotland to be disturbed.[34]

The West Berliners, however, were extremely disappointed by this pointed calmness of their allies. (Of course many East Berliners and GDR citizens were also disappointed, but unlike their compatriots in the West, they had to keep these feelings to themselves.) A few days after the closure of the borders the Mayor of West Berlin, Willy Brandt, sent a telegram to President Kennedy, in which he clearly spelt out the West Berliners' disappointment. Amongst the population there were already serious "doubts about the three Western Powers' ability and determination to react." Kennedy may have been annoyed by the undiplomatic and imperious tone of the telegram, but he recognised the necessity of a tough stance in order not to damage

› Moderne Grenze ‹

1 Betonplattenwand mit oder ohne Rohr
2 Metallgitterzaun
3 Kontrollstreifen [KS]
4 Beleuchtungsanlage
5 Kfz-Graben
6 Linie der vorderen Begrenzung des
    Grenzpostens
7 Kolonnenweg
8 Hundelaufanlage
9 Signalgerät   12 Schutzbunker
10 Scheinwerfer   13 Kontaktzaun
11 Beobachtungsturm   14 Wildfangzaun

Gebiet der Grenzsicherungs-
oder Pioniertechnischen Anlagen

Siehe Kapitel „Moderne Grenze" Seite 6

Sketch representation of the border installation from a GDR border guards' textbook, cynically entitled "modern border"

the trust that the Berliners and the (West-) Germans as a whole had put in the leadership of the Americans. So a few days after the building of the wall he risked a direct confrontation with the Soviets by sending a military convoy of 1500 GIs down the motorway from West Germany to West Berlin. After they had passed unmolested through the GDR border crossing points, it was clear that the Kremlin and the GDR government were not interested in aggravating the situation either. At the same time the US Vice-President, Lyndon B. Johnson landed at Tempelhof airport and was enthusiastically greeted by the West Berliners. At last the USA had nailed their colours to the mast.

A few weeks after the border had been closed, at the end of October 1961, one of those East-West confrontations described in the opening chapter occurred at Checkpoint Charlie. For three days US and Soviet tanks were lined up there, with their gun turrets pointing right at each other. Finally, they retreated again on direct instructions from Moscow and Washington. The trigger for this "tank duel" was the attempt by the SED leadership to restrict the rights of the Western Allies in the whole of Berlin by demanding that American Officers show their identity cards when crossing the sector border. The Americans flatly refused to do this, as it would have meant an inadmissible infringement of the Allies' right to freedom of movement in all four sectors. By sending in their tanks the Americans were unequivocally demonstrating that they would claim this right – to move freely and without controls in the whole of Berlin even after the building of the Wall – with the use of weapons if necessary. Finally Moscow and East Berlin had to accept this freedom of movement.

In Berlin the territories were marked out and the border was cemented with a wall. Both power blocks had in effect recognised their respective spheres of influence within Europe: the West the existence of communist states in East and Middle Europe, including the GDR and East Berlin and the East the presence of the Western Allies in West Berlin. Now Berlin could return to some sort of precarious normality, although of course for the people it was a bitter normality in the shadow of the Wall, under the conditions of a divided city.

The main aim of the GDR government was to prevent any escapes from East to West. The border installations were therefore continually strengthened over the coming months and years. At first the barriers consisted of barbed wire and fences. The first parts of the Wall were erected in mid-August 1961, using concrete blocks and bricks with barbed wire along the top to stop people climbing over it. After some refugees succeeded in driving vehicles through this 30 centimetre thick "Wall of the 1st Generation", (there were four extension stages, "Wall generations" between 1961 and 1989) they were replaced by sheets of concrete layered on top of each other. Watch towers, initially made of wood and later of concrete, were erected along the border and a convoy road was laid down for patrol vehicles. From 1968 the Wall consisted of square sheets of concrete with piping on top of it. This "Wall of the 3rd Generation" was gradually replaced by the "4th Generation" from 1976 onwards. This consisted of concrete segments measuring 3.6 metres by 1.2 metres with 40 centimetre piping along the top. A total of 45,000 pieces of these segments of Wall surrounded West Berlin until 1989.

A tense peace

As painful as the Wall was for those immediately affected, for the time being it still marked the end of an epoch in which the four sector city represented a permanent trouble spot from where, since 1948, the acute risk of war had emanated more than once. In Berlin, at least, the balance of power between the East and West seemed clear, despite – or perhaps because of – the unnatural division of a whole city by concrete and barbed wire. Of course the Cold War was not over, but rather its main focus moved to other regions of the world.

To Cuba, for example, where since 1959 a social revolutionary movement ruled led by the political hothead, Fidel Castro, and went about building a socialist state right on America's doorstep. When the Soviet Union went on to install the first medium range rockets on Cuba in the summer of 1962, the USA felt that this was a threat to their security and therefore vigorously demanded the withdrawal of the rockets. The crisis came to a head in October 1962 when Soviet freighters with more rockets moved towards Cuba, unmistakeably threatening Washington with a massive military hit should they be actually set up. Kennedy's toughness and determination had an effect. Before things could come the worst, on 28th October, Khrushchev gave the order to turn round. In the weeks that followed all Soviet weapons were withdrawn from Cuba. In exchange the Americans dismantled their rockets in Turkey, which had posed a threat to large areas of the Soviet Union.[35]

Berlin was even present in the Cuba crisis. US President Kennedy wrote to the British Prime Minister Macmillan: "I don't need to point out to you the possible connection between this dangerous step by Khrushchev (the installation of rockets on Cuba, T.F.) and Berlin." Kennedy was actually convinced that Khrushchev's main reason for using Cuba as a threat was to achieve concessions from the Western Allies in Berlin, perhaps even their withdrawal from West Berlin. According to the information we now have, Kennedy was making an error of judgement here. Khrushchev had already accepted the fact that there was nothing to be done about the presence of the Western Allies in West Berlin in 1961/62.[36] In Cuba he was not concerned with Berlin, but with Moscow's strategic position in Latin America and Asia.

In Asia – or to be more precise, in Vietnam – a new focus of attention in the Cold War was developing during those same years that the Berliners were having to come to terms with the consequences of the Cold War. In 1960, when the Vietcong, backed by Moscow and Peking, advanced further and further into pro-West South Vietnam, US President Dwight D. Eisenhower increased military support for the South Vietnamese government. After Kennedy's assassination in November 1963, his successor, Lyndon B. Johnson continued this policy of intervention with aiming for a "roll back" of the communist troops. Following the incident in the Gulf of Tonkin in August 1964 – which may partly have been staged by the Americans – when US warships were attacked by North Vietnamese speedboats, the conflict grew into a full-scale war. The numbers of US troops in South Vietnam was increased from 75,000 to 540,000 men between 1965 and 1968. However, as is well-known, despite a massive military effort which included highly questionable operations, such as the defoliation of whole tracts of land using "Agent Orange", which was also deadly poisonous for human beings and the expansion of hostilities to Cambodia, which went against international law, the Americans were unable to defeat the

Vietcong. Indeed, the Western Powers in Vietnam suffered a painful defeat and had to evacuate their last troops and embassy staff from the South Vietnamese capital of Saigon (today Hoh Chi Minh City).

Escape and escape aid

Despite the constant improvements to the border installations GDR citizens kept trying again and again to escape over the Wall into West Berlin. Over 100 of them paid for their attempt with their lives. On 24th August 1961, the 24 year old tailor, Günter Litfin was shot dead by a border guard in Humboldthain, close to Friedrichstraße Station, when he tried to swim across to West Berlin. He was the first refugee to be shot at the Wall. The GDR border guards were instructed to prevent any escapes or "border breakthroughs" at all costs, even if it meant using a gun. The SED regime stubbornly refused to admit to the existence of an "order to shoot" on the Wall and the inner German border. However, in reality this was more or less the case. Even the GDR border law of 25th March 1982 contained an actual order to shoot in the case of escape attempts. In paragraph 27 it states: "… when using (a gun) a person's life should, if possible, be spared." But only "if possible". Basically, in cases of escape attempts, a gun was to be used recklessly.

According to the latest research, a total of at least 99 people were shot dead or met their deaths in their bid to escape. A further 25 people were shot dead or died by accident, without having any intention to escape. Eight border guards were killed on service, most of them by colleagues who were deserting – two of whom were likewise shot.

The last Wall refugee to be shot dead was the 22 year old Chris Gueffroy who died in a barrage of fire from border guards on 5th February 1989. Four weeks later, a 32 year old man died in his bid to conquer the Wall in a hot air balloon.

No other event demonstrated as drastically to the world the monstrous nature of the Wall as the agonizing death of the 18 year old refugee, Peter Fechter. On 17th August 1962, near Checkpoint Charlie. Fechter wanted to escape to the West together with a friend. While the friend managed to climb over the Wall, Peter Fechter was hit by several bullets and lay on the Eastern side of the Wall. Despite his desperate pleas the GDR border guards refused to help and the seriously wounded Fechter bled to death. An hour later his lifeless body was carried away by the guards. Numerous people on the western side, including journalists and television cameras, had had to watch the whole event in helpless fury. Even a US Officer refused to come to the aid of the refugee lying on the eastern side, stating that he did not have the authority to do so. Peter Fechter was thus victim of a political and military situation in which the Americans and Soviets faced each other with furtive rigidity. Peter Fechter's death caused the West Berlin politicians to have a certain change of heart. The fatal restraint of the Americans had shown that it would be first and foremost the task of the Germans and Berlin politicians to remove at least part of the terror of the Wall. It was above all the Mayor of West Berlin, Willy Brandt and his close friends, Egon Bahr and Heinrich Albertz, who sought political means of making the Wall more "permeable".

The building of the War did not mean that the escape movement came to an abrupt end, just many GDR citizens naturally did not stop wishing for a life without orders and repressions. However, after 13th August 1961 it had become much more difficult and dangerous to turn this wish into reality.

Nevertheless, more and more people were prepared to put their lives on the line in order to flee to West Berlin. As the border installations were being constantly strengthened, this required an increasing amount of daring and imagination. In 1962 about 2,300 people succeeded in getting through the Wall and the border installations. In 1963 it was only 640 and in the following year just 300 and in 1968 only 46. Between August 1961 and November 1989, a total of 5,075 people managed to flee to West Berlin. The total number of refugees from the GDR, who escaped over the Wall, on the inner German border and via third countries, amounts to just over 40,000.[37]

Many of these escapes would not have succeeded if a few, mainly young, people had not declared their own private "war" against the SED regime and the Wall immediately after the border had been sealed. These escape helpers, who were both imaginative and brave, prepared the way out to the West for numerous GDR citizens. In doing so, they used a great variety of methods and mostly knew that they were putting their own lives at risk.

In the first weeks after the border was closed, so-called "passport missions" were very successful, where foreign students went to East Berlin and handed their passports over to people who wanted to escape. Alternatively, passports from the West were smuggled in for refugees who resembled the actual owner of the passport. When the GDR border authorities perfected the checks on foreigners and West Germans at the beginning of 1962, this method of escape was "scotched". Other ways had to be found, for example under the ground.

1962–63 was the big time for tunnel building. The first spectacular tunnel escape succeeded on January 24th 1962, After several weeks of digging in the

Peter Fechter lies bleeding to death by the Wall

On the day the Wall was put up, people living on Bernauer Straße fled from their homes which stood directly on the border

Oranienburger Chaussee in the north of Berlin, 28 people crawled through under the border installations into the West. In the spring, not far from the same place, 12 people, most of them pensioners, dug a 32 metre long and 1.75 metre high tunnel in which they were able to "walk unbent into freedom", as the 81 year old leader proudly declared after their successful mission.

On Bernauer Straße a group of 41 men worked for months on a tunnel over 150 metres long, which ran from West Berlin into the East Berlin territory. There were a great many difficulties and problems to overcome, including water bursting into the tunnel, before 27 women, men and two small children could crawl into the West on 14th September 1962. The television cameras were there to film the emerging escapees because, much to the annoyance of some of their comrades-in-arms,

the tunnel builders had sold the exclusive media rights for 12,000 US dollars to the American broadcasting company, NBC, in order to pay for the tunnel which had cost a great deal in time and materials.

In October 1964, 57 GDR citizens even managed an escape through a tunnel, which escape helpers, mainly students, had dug at a depth of 12 metres from under the cellar of a closed-down bakery in Bernauer Straße 145 metres into East Berlin. When the tunnel was discovered shortly before the mission was complete, there was an exchange of shots and one of the border guards was accidentally killed by one of his fellow guards.

Two escape helpers were also killed by shots from border guards during other tunnel missions.

There were a total of about 40 attempted tunnel escapes in Berlin. However, many projects failed because the money ran out, the technical problems proved insurmountable or because the tunnel builders were betrayed by Stasi spies.

Initially the escape aiders enjoyed the strong support of the population and good political will, but from 1963 onwards this changed, at least as far as official politics was concerned. After the West Berlin Senate had begun their "politics of small steps" *(Politik der kleinen Schritte),* spectacular escape missions were increasingly viewed as disruptive.

People even tried to cross the Wall in the air and on the water. One evening in July 1965, a professional economist from Leipzig secretly met up with his wife and their 9 year old son in the toilets of the *Haus der Ministerien* (today the Federal Finance Ministry). When darkness fell they climbed up on to the roof of the building complex which stood right next to the Wall. The man slung a hammer attached to a cable over the Wall. On the western side escape helpers bound a steel cable to it which the escapees pulled up and fastened to a flagpole. First his son and wife and then the man himself glided across this improvised "cableway" into West Berlin.

Others tried to get into the West by swimming; as four young people succeeded in doing in the summer of 1988 very near to the Reichstag. They were cheered on by people standing on the Western side and filmed by a camera team which happened to be there.

In June 1962, 12 escapees even hijacked a whole pleasure steamer on the Spree near the Oberbaum Bridge and steered it into West Berlin waters, despite being shot at by border guards.

However, every successful escape attempt meant that the border installations were increasingly strengthened and extended. Over the years, it became more and more difficult and dangerous to escape.

Living with the Wall

First visits from relatives

In 1962 it must have been clear to even the keenest anti-communists that it would be impossible to remove the Wall so soon. This was even particularly evident to the Western Allies, for whom, as their spontaneous reactions to the building of the Wall showed, the cementing up of the division was obviously preferable to the permanent threat of war in Berlin. The West Berlin Mayor, Willy Brandt, had therefore already issued a new watchword in September 1961: if the Wall cannot be removed, everything must be done to ensure that it is as permeable as possible.

Thus began the "policy of small steps" that were meant to bring some relief to the people of Berlin. However, they had to wait for over two years for the first signs of progress. After lengthy negotiations, a pass permit agreement was put in place for Christmas 1963. Between 19th December 1963 and 5th January 1964, West Berliners were allowed for the first time for two years to visit their relatives in the eastern part of the city. Before going, they had to go through a complicated procedure, which involved waiting for hours outside the pass permit issue offices in West Berlin. At the border crossing points there were tearful reunions. An elderly woman from West Berlin described her feelings: "We used to sit down together every day. After the Wall was built I am all alone in West Berlin. I have needed a lot of strength to survive for the past two years. ... I have queued for three days to get the three pass permits. I will queue again, even if it takes longer."[38] Over Christmas 1963, a total of 1,242,000 day pass permits were issued. For the following two years pass permits regulations were also negotiated for the Christmas period.

There were four pass permit agreements altogether, the last one for Whitsun 1966. Further visiting regulations broke down due to demands by the GDR that the West did not want to agree to, in order to avoid any semblance of recognising the SED regime under international law.

In 1964, however, "a pass permit office for urgent family matters" was established for West Berliners. This meant that they could apply for a pass permit for births, marriages, life-threatening illnesses or the death of a close relative. This regulation was only valid for visits originating from West Berlin. For the people of East Berlin the Wall remained impenetrable, at least until they reached retirement age.

An agreement for Berlin

After the last pass permit regulation at Whitsun 1966, long years followed during which the Wall seemed impassable even for the West Berlin population. Berlin was paralysed on the front lines of the Cold War and the people in both halves of the city increasingly lived separate lives. However, the debate in and around Berlin started moving again at the end of the 1960s in the wake of the politics of détente. A socialist-liberal coalition government with Willy Brandt as Federal Chancellor had been in power in Bonn in 1969 and was trying to break up the front lines of the Cold War through negotiations. The other capitals in the West were also in favour of détente. Meanwhile in Moscow, Khrushchev had been deposed by Leonid

Living in the shadow of the Wall

Brezhnev, who was admittedly anything but a political reformer, but in foreign policy he wanted peace, in Europe at least. (It was one of the mechanisms of the Cold War that almost parallel to the détente in Berlin and mid-Europe the conflict escalated elsewhere, in this case in South Asia.)

For Berlin and its population on both sides of the Wall this process of détente brought distinct improvements. It almost seemed as if the conflicting parties in the long dispute about Berlin, that had so often brought the world to the edge of war, had grown tired.

The constant arguments about access routes and visiting regulations were to be finally settled. In March 1970, the ambassadors of the four victorious powers sat down together round the negotiating table for the first time in decades in the Allied Control Council building with the desire for unity. After 18 months of struggle the "Four Power Agreement" was ceremonially signed on 3rd September 1971 in West Berlin. It was the first governmental agreement between the four powers since the beginning of the Cold War in 1946–47 and signalled the beginning of a new era for Berlin. At least in this Cold War theatre practical sense had prevailed over ideological dogmatism, because in the interests of pragmatic solutions, disputed questions of status, for example the link between West Berlin and the Federal Republic, had been excluded. The Four Power Agreement and the Transit Treaty agreed directly between Bonn and East Berlin on 17th December 1971 made things much easier for people. Moscow and the GDR promised to keep the access routes to and from Berlin permanently open. The harassment that had occurred on the transit motorways, and sometimes included hours of waiting, was over.

Visitors from West Berlin hurry to meet their relatives on the Oberbaum Bridge

Most important was that from now on the visiting regulations were for an unlimited period. West Berliners could apply for visits to East Berlin for a total of 30 days per year. The GDR authorities set up five "offices for visits and travel" in West Berlin whereby the West insisted that applications would only be received there. The actual paperwork had to completed in East Berlin because the West Berlin Senate would not tolerate any sovereign acts by the SED regime – for example the approval of travel permits – on West Berlin territory. These "offices for visits and travel" were a piece of the GDR in West Berlin. They were furnished and decorated with the charm of all GDR offices in which the applicants were "admitted" with bureaucratic correctness. In 1984 the number of possible visiting days was increased to 45 per year and in 1988 a "multiple entitlement permit" for a total of ten visits was introduced which reduced the tiresome waiting in the application offices.

Several hundred thousand West Berliner made use of these new visiting regulation. The average annual number of day visits to East Berlin totalled over 3.1 million.

Not least, the high number of visitors from the West soon became a headache to the GDR state security and the border guards because they meant inevitable contacts and information from the West which the authorities wanted to keep from the GDR population.

In 1980 the GDR leadership thought up a means of controlling the stream of visitors from West Berlin by introducing the "minimum exchange". In 1972 in order to cross the border the West Berliners had to exchange 5 DM at a rate of 1:1. In 1980 this amount was increased fivefold to 25 DM. By the following year the number of

Border controls at the Dreilinden checkpoint on entry into West Berlin

day visitors had already fallen by about a third to 1.7 million and in 1983 it fell to its lowest level at 1.5 million day visits. By 1988 the number gradually climbed again to over two million.

Normal state of emergency

When the Four Power Agreement came into force in June 1972 a completely new chapter in the Cold War began in and around Berlin.

The four sector city stopped being a permanent trouble spot where a military conflict between the super powers could flare up at any time.

The people in both halves of the city gradually came to terms with the life in the shadow of the Wall which continued to involve many unpleasant aspects, shortages and hardships, above all for the people of East Berlin, but which had become less

oppressive on the whole since the efforts to achieve détente. Willy Brandt's "policy of small steps" had actually led to the Wall becoming more permeable, at least from West to East.

At the beginning of the 1970s things must have been for many people in East Berlin rather as the GDR writer Günter de Bruyn described in his memoirs: "… the provisional had obtained solid contours; … In the long run it was necessary to get by, to found a family, to have children … not to stand out by making a bad impression. … I could see myself getting used to things. My opinion of the Wall remained unchanged, but I learnt to adjust to the new conditions and not to be permanently angry about the restriction on freedom". But the pain kept returning. It sufficed to see the "improvements to the border installations, the searchlights on the Marschall Bridge, which were meant to

Patrol at Potsdamer Platz S-Bahn station. Trains run from West to West without stopping

Documented "provocative behaviour by the enemy" from the archives of the GDR border troops

prevent a view of the Reichstag or the new maps and street plans which just blanked out West Berlin in white as if the world ended at the border".[39]

Erich Honecker, who had replaced Walter Ulbricht in 1971 as leader of the SED, did his bit to promote this "habituation" (Günter de Bruyn) for a large number of people in East Berlin and the GDR. Pension schemes, improved provision of food and consumer goods, ambitious housing programmes and other things contributed towards making living conditions East Berlin noticeably better. At least, provided people managed to ignore the restrictions on freedom and the repressions by the SED regime.

However this phase of relative "upturn" in East Berlin and the GDR only lasted until the beginning of the 1980s. After that, the immobility of the planned economy,

a lack of innovative power, rapidly rising state debts etc. all meant that shortages and slack began to determine daily life more and more. In East Berlin and elsewhere the disrepair of the housing from 1981/82 onwards symbolised the decay of the State and of society. The government's reaction consisted mainly in strengthened repressions against any form of opposition.

In the meantime, in West Berlin both the population and official policy seemed to be less and less interested in the conditions in East Berlin. It was, so to speak, the drawback to the détente in and around Berlin. A certain indifference followed the angry confrontation in the "rivalry of the systems".

Other questions and problems increasingly determined peoples' thoughts and actions; questions about lifestyle, increase in wealth, culture and how to spend leisure.

John F. Kennedy giving his speech in front of the Schöneberg Town Hall on 26th June 1963

It soon seemed to West Berliners that reality outside their city only began again beyond "Helmstedt", in other words once they had got through the transit route through the GDR. West Berlin developed into a social and political "biotope" whose island situation brought considerable advantages for large groups of the population. In the wake of the student movement of the sixties a largely left-orientated (academic) youth scene developed which sat in communes in old apartments and discussed the solutions to world problems, but mostly excluded the conditions only a few kilometres away. However, it certainly wasn't the most lethargic or the least imaginative who came to Berlin from West Germany. They came to "test themselves" there and among other things to take social problems in hand, as they did in the 1980s by squatting in hundreds of houses which had been left empty by speculators.

The majority of the population regarded this activity with disapproval but also a certain calmness whilst they made themselves a comfortable life in the "shadow of the Wall".

The fact that daily life in West Berlin was relatively easy, despite all the adversities, had a lot to do with the political and economic guarantees provided by the Western Allies and the Federal Government. West Berlin's situation was precarious in times of détente, too. It was reassuring for West Berliners to have the world power of the USA and its allies behind them and it was nice to have half the West Berlin budget financed by Bonn.

To exaggerate, one might say that in fact the Cold War only lasted in Berlin until 1972. That is, if it hadn't been for 9th November 1989 when the fall of the Wall brought Berlin back on to the centre stage. It was here that the rapid collapse of the

The American President Ronald Reagan in front of the Brandenburg Gate on 12th June 1987

Soviet Empire was so plain to see – and with it the end of the Cold War in general.

"Mister Gorbachev ..."

In 1963 the most powerful men in the world and the main adversaries in the Cold War US President John F. Kennedy and the Soviet State and Party leader, Nikita S. Khrushchev had visited Berlin shortly after one another. Each one in "his" half of course. Kennedy had given his legendary speech then, in June 1963, in front of the Schöneberg Town Hall, which ended with the famous declaration "Ich bin ein Berliner!"

At the end of the 1980s US President Ronald Reagan and the Soviet Party Leader Mikhail S. Gorbachev, came to Berlin shortly after one another. In front of the Brandenburg Gate, right by the Berlin Wall, Reagan asked Gorbachev (in his absence) to "tear down the Wall". "General Secretary Gorbachev, if you seek peace, … then come here to this gate! Mr Gorbachev, open this gate! Mr Gorbachev, tear down this wall!".

The GDR border troops had set up huge oudspeakers on the other side of the Wall to drown the speech with music.

The end of the Cold War

Reagan was ridiculed at the time by large numbers of the public for this pathetic demand, because hardly anyone imagined how relevant it was to the current situation and how quickly the Brandenburg Gate would be open again.

At the end of the 1980s things had really started fermenting in the GDR and all over the Eastern Bloc – and hardly anyone in the West seemed to have noticed. Opposition groups voiced louder and louder criticism on repression, a failing economy, the militarisation of society and environmental pollution. In the summer of 1987 there was a direct confrontation between youths and the People's Police, when 4,000 pop music fans were brutally forced back when they wanted to listen to a pop concert near the Brandenburg Gate that was taking place on the other side of the Wall. Choruses chanted "The Wall must go" (*"Die Mauer muss weg"*) and "Gorbi, Gorbi", because in 1987–88 many opposition groups in the GDR hoped for support from the Soviet Party Leader who was vigorously pushing forward his reform policies in Moscow under the banners of "Glasnost" and "Perestroika". Those in power in the GDR were not thinking about reforms but about more about tougher repressions.

In the summer of 1989 pressure on the SED regime increased. In Poland and in Hungary the Communist Parties had already had to cede some of their power and

Günter Schabowski (right) at the historic press conference of 9ᵗʰ November 1989

The borders are open. Trabbis and rejoicing crowds on Bornholmer Straße

tens of thousands of GDR citizens had used their holiday travel to Hungary and Czechoslovakia to flee to the West. They either took the direct route across the Hungarian border or fled first to the Federal German Embassies to force their exit into the West.

In the face of this mass exodus and emigration by GDR citizens it was no use any longer when in autumn 1989 younger and somewhat less stubborn SED politicians like Egon Krenz, Hans Modrow or Günter Schabowski replaced the old guard surrounding Erich Honecker and Stasi leader Erich Mielke. The overwhelming majority had had enough of the SED State whose end was actually sealed by the fall of the Wall on 9th November.

At an historic press conference on the evening of 9th November 1989 Günter Schabowski had wrongly read out a new travel regulation without realising what this would trigger. "Private journeys abroad can be applied for without preconditions – having to state reasons or relationships. Permission will be granted at short notice". Evidently Schabowski did not know what he was hesitantly reading out there. A journalist enquired: "When does this come into force?" Schabowski rummaged around helplessly in his papers. "As far as I know, it comes into ... straightaway, immediately."

The "Tagesschau" television news main story at 8 p.m. was "GDR opens border". Now there was no turning back. In East Berlin thousands of people streamed to the border crossing points and demanded with increasing force that the barriers be lifted. The border officials had neither information nor orders. In the face of the growing masses of people, the official in charge at the Bornholmer Straße crossing point was the first to decide on his own authority to lift the barrier.

Rejoicing people streamed in their thousands towards West Berlin. Shortly afterwards other crossing points were also open at Invalidenstraße, Checkpoint Charlie and Sonnenallee. After 28 years the Wall had fallen.

This was, in effect, the end of the Cold War in and around Berlin. This end was sealed in October 1990 with the reunification of Germany and Berlin. Four years later in April 1994 the ceremonial farewell to the last Russian troops in Germany took place on the Gendarmenmarkt in the presence of Federal Chancellor Helmut Kohl and the Russian President Boris Jelzin. The American, British and French military, who had protected the "front-line city of Berlin" for over forty years from being taken over by the East, also left their barracks.

Chronology

9 May 1945
Unconditional surrender of Nazi Germany
July 1945
The Americans and the British move into
their sectors
11 July 1945
The first meeting of the Allied Komman-
dantura
August 1945
The French move into their sector
21–22 August 1946
Founding of the SED by uniting the SPD
and the KPD in the Soviet Zone of Occupa-
tion
20 October 1946
The City Council elections
20 June 1948
The introduction of the D-Mark in the three
Western zones of occupation
23 June 1948
Introduction of the Ostmark in the eastern
zone of occupation
24 June 1948 – 12 May 1949
Blockade and airlift
4 December 1948
Founding of the "Free University" in
Berlin-Dahlem
5 December 1948
Elections to the City Council in the three
west sectors. Ernst Reuter becomes Mayor.
23 May 1949
Founding of the Federal Republic of Germany
7 October 1949
Founding of the GDR
May 1952
The road links between West Berlin and the
surrounding countryside are sealed off on
the orders of the GDR government
17 June 1953
People's uprising against the SED regime

27 November 1958
Khrushchev Ultimatum
15 June 1961
Ulbricht announces to the press in East
Berlin: "No-one has he intention of erecting
a wall."
13 August 1961
The building of the Wall begins
25 October 1961
Confrontation between American and
Soviet tanks at Checkpoint Charlie
17 August 1962
Peter Fechter is shot trying to escape over
the Wall and bleeds to death in the border
strip
26 June 1963
President Kennedy visits West Berlin
19 December 1963
The first pass permit agreement comes into
force and lasts until 5 January 1964
1964
Three further pass permit agreements
follow until the middle of 1966
3 May 1971
Honecker replaces Ulbricht as SED Party
leader
3 September 1971
The Four Power Agreement on Berlin
17 December 1971
Signing of the Transit Treaty between the
Federal Republic and the GDR
9 November 1989
Fall of the Wall
3 October 1990
GDR joins the constitution of the Federal
Republic of Germany, Reunification
1994
Withdrawal of the last Soviet troops from
Germany

Key locations in Cold War Berlin

1. Checkpoint Charlie
2. Museum at Checkpoint Charlie
3. Karl-Marx-Allee (until 1961 Stalinallee)
4. Wall Memorial, Bernauer Straße
5. Allied Control Building,
   containing Air Safety Control Centre
6. Schöneberg Town Hall
7. RIAS
8. Allied Kommandantura
9. US Military Headquarters
10. CIA Headquarters
11. Free University FU
12. Allied Museum
13. Soviet Headquarters in Karlshorst
14. KGB Headquarters
15. Tempelhof Airport (Airlift Memorial)
16. Gatow Airport
17. Tegel Airport
18. Hansaviertel (Hansa District)
19. Glienicker Bridge

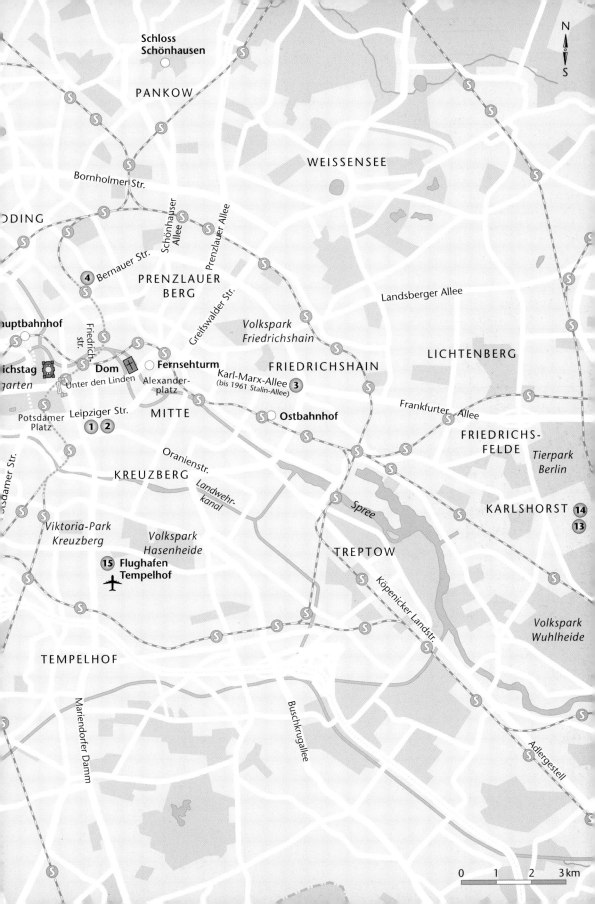

N

Schloss
Schönhausen

PANKOW

WEISSENSEE

Bornholmer Str.

⊘DING

Bernauer Str.

④

Schönhauser Allee

Prenzlauer Allee

PRENZLAUER
BERG

Landsberger Allee

Greifswalder Str.

Volkspark
Friedrichshain

LICHTENBERG

Hauptbahnhof

Friedrich-
str.

Dom

Fernsehturm

Unter den Linden

FRIEDRICHSHAIN

richstag

Alexander-
platz

Karl-Marx-Allee
(bis 1961 Stalin-Allee)

③

Frankfurter   Allee

FRIEDRICHS-
FELDE

garten

Potsdamer
Platz

Leipziger Str.

MITTE

Ostbahnhof

Tierpark
Berlin

sdamer Str.

① ②

Oranienstr.

KREUZBERG

Landwehr-
kanal

Spree

KARLSHORST ⑭

⑬

Viktoria-Park
Kreuzberg

Volkspark
Hasenheide

TREPTOW

⑮ Flughafen
Tempelhof

Köpenicker Landstr.

Volkspark
Wuhlheide

TEMPELHOF

Mariendorfer Damm

Buschkrugallee

Adlergestell

0   1   2   3 km

Notes

1 Wyden, Peter, Die Mauer war unser Schicksal, Berlin 1995, p. 120

2 Quoted from Beschloss, Michael, Powergame Kennedy und Chruschtschow – Krisenjahre 1960–1963, Düsseldorf 1991, p. 281

3 Quoted from Leonhard, Wolfgang, Die Revolution entlässt ihre Kinder. München ⁵1982, p. 317

4 Ribbe, Wolfgang (Hg.), Geschichte Berlins, Bd. 2, München 1987, p. 1050

5 Bouvier, Beatrix, Ausgeschaltet! Sozialdemokraten in der Sowjetischen Besatzungszone und in der DDR 1945–1953, Bonn 1996

6 Ribbe, Wolfgang (Hg.), Geschichte Berlins, München 1987, Bd. 2, p. 1043

7 Stöver, Bernd, Der Kalte Krieg. Geschichte eines radikalen Zeitalters, 1947–1991, München 2007, p. 92

8 Clay's letter to Sokolowski, quoted from Berlin. Quellen und Dokumente, I/2, Nr. 755, p. 1334

9 On the complex problem of currency reform in Berlin, cf. Wolff, Michael W., Die Währungsreform in Berlin 1948/49, Berlin 1991

10 Bennett, Jack O., 40 000 Stunden am Himmel, Berlin 1982, p. 200

11 Churchill to a high ranking official in the British Foreign Office at the end of June 1953, quoted from Larres, Klaus, Großbritannien und der 17. Juni 1953, in: Kleßmann, Bristoph/Stöver, Bernd, 1953 – Krisenjahr des Kalten Krieges in Europa, Köln 1999, S. 172

12 Quoted from Large, David Clay, Berlin. Biographie einer Stadt, München 2002, p. 409

13 Ibid., p. 407

14 Bailey, George/Kondraschow, Sergej A./Murphy, David E., Die unsichtbare Front. Der Krieg der Geheimdienste im geteilten Berlin, Berlin 1997, p. 259

15 Ibid., p. 159

16 Quoted from Flemming, Thomas/Ulrich, Bernd, Vor Gericht. Deutsche Prozesse in Ost und West nach 1945, Berlin 2005, p. 21

17 Quoted from Lemke, Michael, Die Berlin-Krise 1958 bis 1963, Berlin 1995, p. 47

18 Dokumente zur Berlin-Frage 1944–1966, hrsg. von der deutschen Gesellschaft für Auswärtige Politik, München 1962, p. 315

19 Khruschev Ultimatum, quoted from Dokumente zur Berlin-Frage 1944–1966, München 1962, p. 314f

20 Ibid., p. 318

21 Strauß, Franz Josef, Erinnerungen, Berlin 1989, p. 388 and Stöver, Bernd, Der Kalte Krieg, München 2007, p. 136

22 Steininger, Rolf, Der Mauerbau. Die Westmächte und Adenauer in der Berlinkrise 1958–1963, München 2001, p. 99

23 Macmillan in a letter to US President Dwight D. Eisenhower, 23.6.1959, quoted from Steininger, Rolf, Der Mauerbau, München 2001, p. 124

24 Hobsbawn, Eric, Age of Extremes. The Short Twenty Century 1914–1991, London 1995, p. 243

25 The division of Germany also meant that after 1949 several hundred thousand people from the Federal Republic settled in the GDR. The latest estimates put the number at 603,000 between 1949 and 1989. (Other studies estimate about 400,000 such migrants. Wendt, H., Von der Massenflucht zur Binnenwanderung, in: Geographische Rundschau 46/1994, p. 136–140; p. 137; Schmelz, A., Politik und Migration im geteilten Deutschland während des Kalten Krieges, West-Ost-Migration in die DDR, Opladen 2002, p. 39) The reasons for this migration from West to East were many and diverse, but were mainly to do with family or career.

26 Quoted from Lemke, Michael, Die Berlin-Krise 1958 bis 1963, Berlin 1995, p. 49

27 Quoted from Foreign Relations of the United States, Vol. XIV, Berlin Crisis, 1961–1962, Washington 1993, p. 98

28 Quoted from Wyden, Peter, Die Mauer war unser Schicksal, Berlin 1995, p. 28

29 Quoted from Beschloss, Michael, Powergame, Düsseldorf 1991, p. 242

30 Khrushchev at a meeting with McCloy on 27th July 1961 in the Black Sea resort of Stoschi, quoted from Steininger, Rolf, Der Mauerbau, München 2001, p. 230

31 Rostow, Walt, The Diffusion of Power. An Essay in Recent History, New York 1972, p. 231

32 Kwizinskij, Julij, Vor dem Sturm, Berlin 1993, p. 179 (in 1961 Kwizinskij was a close associate of the Soviet Ambassador Mikhail Perwuchin)

33 Quoted from Beschloss, Powergame, Düsseldorf 1991, p. 281

34 Judt, Tony, Geschichte Europas von 1945 bis zur Gegenwart, München 2006, p. 287

35 Stöver, Bernd, Der Kalte Krieg, München 2007, p. 279f

36 Judt, Tony, Geschichte Europas von 1945 bis zur Gegenwart, München 2006, p. 288

37 Hertle, Hans Hermann, Die Berliner Mauer – Monument des Kalten Krieges, Berlin 2007, p. 57

38 "Tagesspiegel", 25.12.1963

39 de Bruyn, Günter, Vierzig Jahre. Ein Lebensbericht, Frankfurt a. M. ²1996, p. 110